"THE WAY" ("THE WAY")

DATA LINK

SIAC

DAMIANI

Damiani
via Zanardi, 376
40131 Bologna, Italy
t. +39 051 63 56 811
f. +39 051 63 47 188
info@damianieditore.com
www.damianieditore.com

Gordon de Vries Studio, LLC
www.gordondevriesstudio.com
info@gordondevriesstudio.com

ISBN 978-88-6208-231-0

Printed in May 2012 by Grafiche Damiani, Bologna, Italy
Distributed in the United States by D.A.P./Distributed Art Publishers Inc., www.artbook.com

10 9 8 7 6 5 4 3 2 1
First edition

Design by Barbara de Vries @ Gordon de Vries Studio

Cover: Steel courtyard walls, Smith and Thompson Studio, 1998
Endpapers: Planning studies for the Philippines Housing Competition, 1975
Next page: Smith and Thompson Residence, East Hampton, NY, 2011

QUALITIES of DURATION

QUALITIES of DURATION

The Architecture of Phillip Smith and Douglas Thompson

by Alastair Gordon

Contents

A Circle in the Sand

Luis Barragan once said that the unappreciated elements of experience in architecture are magic, amazement, serenity and enchantment.[1] We would like to add feeling, aura, spirit of place and theater. Architecture is a state of mind, a way of tuning one's self to the world and one's presence in it, a preparation for the creative act, for making a plan. The creation of a poetic environment in a natural setting requires a distillation of the given. Over time we came to realize that basic human shelter was the most exciting challenge. We turned away from questions of style and the hierarchies of architectural history to focus on the fundamentals of man and his environment. We began focusing on what Bernard Rudofsky called an "architecture without architects," and this has been the basic theme of our life and work together.

As Louis Sullivan pointed out, architecture is life poetry, not a system of applied logic. It is the profound expression of orderly thought and dialogue, a synthesis that can never be reduced to component elements.[2] We have looked for this poetry in small and ordinary things, whether it be the quality of light, a certain texture or the flow of the seasons. Experientiality is the underlying quality in our work. We are more interested in capturing sensual moments than establishing formal compositions. Harmony is more important than symmetry. Tradition has been of relevance in this search in the same way that space is experienced in a nomadic tent, a circle in the sand, or an Italian galleria. All are to be savored as legacies of our common human experience. In early travels we were struck by how the plans of Mughal Indian palaces were inverted so that connective passageways became the built forms and the resultant voids served as primary spaces. The concept of architecture as a stage set has guided our thinking throughout the years.

Instinct has been the principle determinant in our design process. As architecture proceeds toward greater minimalism there has been less of a distinction between inside and outside, building and landscape, serviced and served, material and immaterial and this brings us back to a new view of our beginning.

We wish to take ourselves and our clients into a collaborative and creative debate to evade prejudices and question habits while celebrating our love for the times in which we live. As you read this book we hope that you may experience the visual record of our work in this light.

Phillip Smith and Douglas Thompson

PAGE 6:
Phillip Smith (left) and Douglas Thompson

OPPOSITE:
Sagaponac Houses,
Sagaponack, NY, 2012

Sod-roofed hives cluster
around a glazed commons in
a wooded landscape.

Qualities of Duration in the Architecture of Phillip Smith and Douglas Thompson

In an age of hyper speed and information overload, the work of Phillip Smith and Douglas Thompson stands out as an oasis of calm. Their buildings are reflective places outside the normal pace of modern urban stress. The two architects work in a gradual (sometimes glacial) hands-on manner in contrast to the current design practice of multitasking and global branding. Their studio on 23rd Street has risen slowly on a corner lot, a tortoise among hares, while the rest of the neighborhood explodes around it, morphing from a rundown manufacturing zone into a fashionable culture zone.

You leave hectic 10th Avenue and enter a quiet, tree shaded courtyard. The branch of a sycamore grows through an oval opening in the wall and the building mounts upwards like a Pueblo village, reflecting the street grid of Manhattan without the gridlock. There are no monolithic statements but, rather, a sequence of deft insertions, accretions, and protrusions that express the project's drawn out evolution. Terraces and porches are interspersed with galleries, workspaces, hidden perches and steel staircases with spidery railings. Smith and Thompson began work on the Jacques Marchais Museum of Tibetan Art in 1995 and, similar to their 23rd Street studio, the project continues to evolve in a series of refinements and additions that nestle into the Staten Island site while echoing the battered forms of traditional Tibetan architecture. "It's our intention to retain the mystery of the existing museum," wrote the architects who have made every effort in their design to enhance the presence of the original 1940s buildings. "Each phase of construction is seen as a resting point or a resolved increment." At the New York Buddhist Church on Riverside Drive, the architects have been working on phased increments of a master plan since 1990.

Smith and Thompson's own weekend house in East Hampton, NY, has been transformed over a twenty-six year period from a tractor barn into a multifaceted space for contemplation and escape. It continues to evolve as a work in progress, a kind of laboratory where the architects can go to see how a new idea plays itself out at full scale. An elevated living room extends to the east on a transparent, floating bridge while a light-catching tower rises above the dining area. A pool house started life as a skeletal steel framework, something like a jungle gym, but slowly morphed into a sod-roofed teahouse.

It's ironic that Smith and Thompson, purveyors of such spatial quietude, were studying architecture at Columbia University during the calamitous year of 1968. The campus was in a state of flux and agitation and the two students bonded over shared interests in urban planning, historic preservation and the indigenous architecture of local cultures. Like so many of the 60's generation, they extended their studies by making architecture pilgrimages of their own, sometimes working for other adherents of slowness like Balkrishna Doshi in Ahmadabad and Fumihiko Maki in Tokyo. They brought what they learned back to New York and established a small, hands-on practice in which they pursued not just the art of architecture but, more importantly, the art of living in the everyday world. "The real master in the art of living makes little distinction between his art and his leisure," said Phil Smith, paraphrasing a Zen Buddhist expression. "He simply pursues his vision of excellence in whatever he does, leaving others to decide whether he is working or playing."

Modernism was presented as a dish served cold, a mass-produced object; shiny and new. Materials, building systems and theories were concerned with speed, flexibility and the testament of constant change. Walter Gropius wrote that architecture should be the "crystal symbol of a new faith" and designed the Bauhaus accordingly. Mies van der Rohe said that less was more, that God resided in the details, while Le Corbusier spoke of a city made for speed. Movies, radio, telephone, high-speed railways and airplanes shrunk the human horizon and brought a sense of urgency and anxiety that intensified with every new wave of technology.

While Smith and Thompson came of age under the influence of "Heroic Modernism" they became increasingly aware of a more inclusive, less didactic branch of the Movement that had been emerging for many years, quietly and off center, by way of Aalto, Kahn, Fuller, Scarpa, Kiesler, Goff, Soleri, and others who saw no collision in the marriage of future and past, no conflict between sensual and functional, anthropological and environmental synergies, or historical insights as applied to a modern, urban matrix. Some of the wisest teachers turned out to be anonymous, untutored architects who built by instinct and common sense, according to basic truths like gravity, symmetry, repetition, necessity, the direction of sun and wind, ceremony and patience. Smith and Thompson turned to such cross-cultural advocates as Bernard Rudofsky who opened their eyes to a world of forgotten vernacular, to an architecture without architects, and Robert Venturi, who brought complexity and contradiction back into discussion.

Their approach grew less monolithic and more cellular as they combined a "soft" modernism with slow, architectural accretion, a kind of built Yoga that derived from sources as varied as the fishermen's cottages of Nantucket, the monasteries of Tibet, the hill towns of Italy and the kampongs of Malaysia. Unlike architecture that arrived with a single notion, an *idée fixe*, this slow baked methodology retained a sense of duration that was shaped primarily by intuition. While working towards an economy of means, they incorporated spatial and textural treatments gathered from their journeys around the world. The intention was never pastiche, however, but rather a reinterpretation and remixing of time-tested values and actions: interweaving, stacking, compression, repetition, necessity, transparency... in a juxtaposition of form, material, texture and proportion.

Smith and Thompson create three-dimensional compositions that reveal the underlying process of design as an art form. Their buildings are built narratives that speak softly over an extended period of time. The work is dedicated to the natural and human spirit of those narratives, repositioning the anthropology of tribal and nomadic cultures into a modern-day condition of stress, high-speed travel and digital communication, offering alternative modes of spatial awareness that sometimes verge on reflection and stasis, even tranquility.

Alastair Gordon

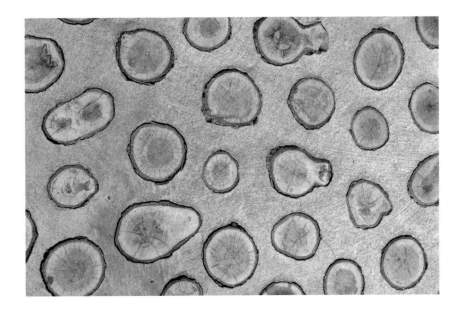

RIGHT:
Floor in Gordon/de Vries Residence

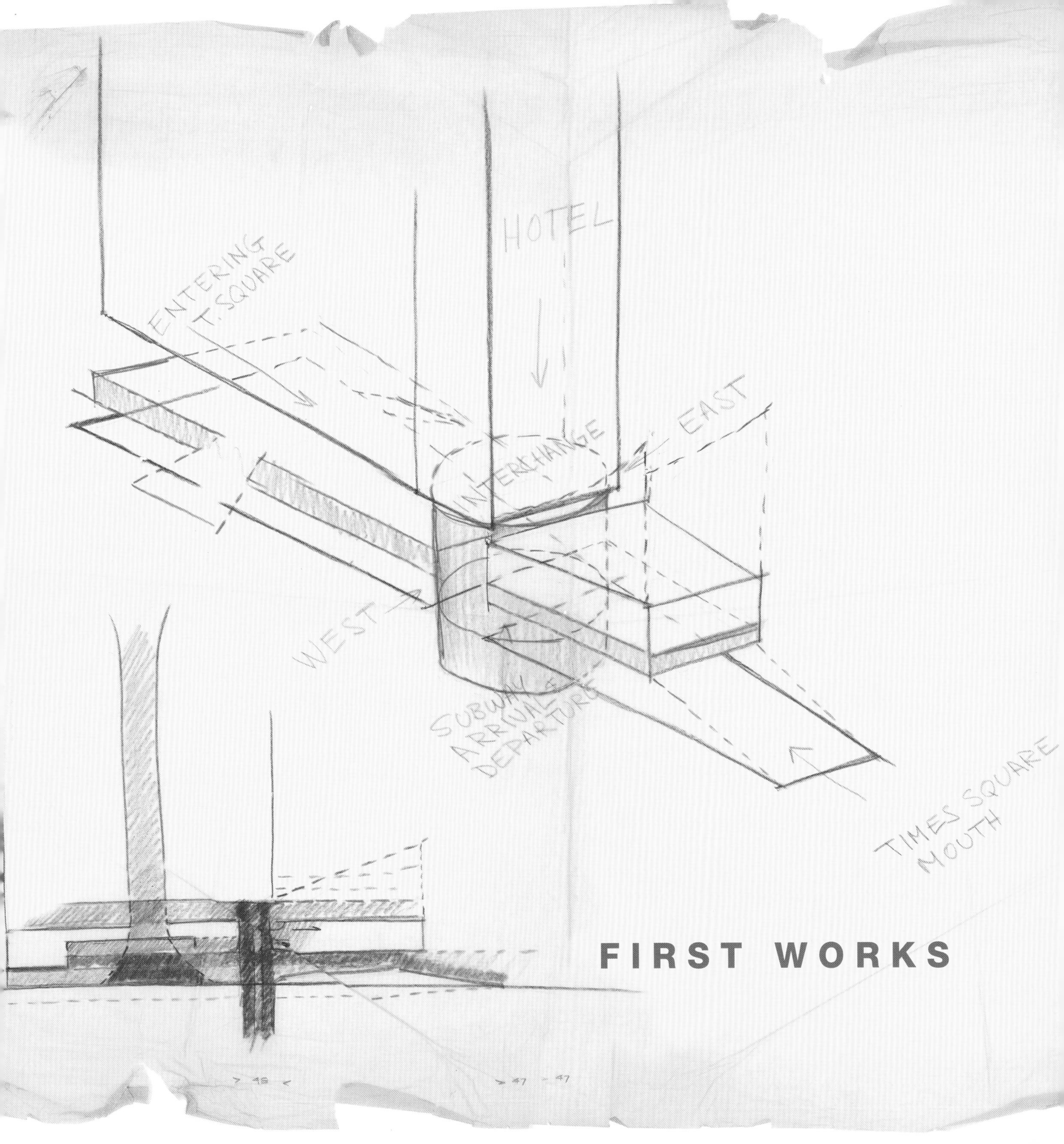

ENTERING T. SQUARE

HOTEL

INTERCHANGE

EAST

WEST

SUBWAY ARRIVAL DEPARTURE

TIMES SQUARE MOUTH

FIRST WORKS

ARCHITECTURE WITHOUT ARCHITECTS
by Bernard Rudofsky

Phillip Smith and Douglas Thompson met in 1966 while attending Columbia University's graduate program in architecture. Smith started the four-year program in 1965 and Thompson in 1966. The following year they were both selected to participate in a "vertical studio" initiated by the chairman of the department, Romaldo Giurgola, to foster critical discourse among second, third, and fourth year students. While collaborating on a project to insert prefabricated housing units into a megastructure, Smith and Thompson discovered that they shared many interests and became friends.

Thompson had done his undergraduate work at Brooklyn College, majoring in Art History, while Smith attended Columbia with a major in Fine Arts and then served four years as an officer in the US Navy before coming back to graduate school. While in the Navy, Smith was able to visit and sketch architectural sites in the Mediterranean including Gaudi's Sagrada Familia in Barcelona and the Casa Malaparte on the Isle of Capri.

They were both inspired by the social urbanism of Team X and Aldo Van Eyck's return to humanistic values in architecture and urban planning. They were equally influenced by Le Corbusier's *Esprit Nouveau* writings and Amédée Ozenfant's *Foundation of Modern Art*. "Corbusier was an inspiration not only for the pure beauty of his projects but for his liberating, yet historically informed plans," says Smith. At the same time they were intrigued by the pop, cartoon-like renderings of the Archigram group in London (Peter Cook, Cedric Price, Ron Herron) who were producing delirious urban fantasies like Plug-In City, Fun Palace, Walking City and Blow-Out Village.

At Columbia, Smith and Thompson came under the mentorship of first-year critic, Peter Prangnell, who encouraged them to develop architectural solutions based on social and environmental concerns that took into account the broader human condition. Prangnell emphasized the need to create a "spirit of place," the importance of movement and circulation, and the development of what he called "in-between spaces" as well as social hierarchies. Another mutually shared influence was *Architecture Without Architects*, a 1964 exhibition at the Museum of Modern Art curated by Bernard Rudofsky, the Austrian-born architect and world-trekking author. Rudofsky's work looked beyond mainstream modernism and showed how indigenous people had as much to teach about form-making as Le Corbusier or Gropius.

While there had been earlier studies on indigenous "native" vernacular, Rudofsky's exhibition and subsequent book featured an eclectic mix of archaic and native shelter, from Italian hill towns to Dogon mud huts, Greek fishing villages to the cave

アイヌ（家）

dwellings of Cappadocia. One grouping called "Movable Architecture" highlighted the lightweight, portable dwellings of Vietnam, Guinea, and Kenya. Another, "Vegetal Roofs," compared a thatched roof in Sudan to the straw roof of a farmhouse in northern Japan, all of which resonated with Smith and Thompson.

Architectural education was turning away from the Bauhaus modernist doctrine and looking more selectively at man, his place in the world and the importance of the natural environment. On Thompson's first day of classes, Prangnell showed *Man of Aran*, the 1934 documentary film by Robert J. Flaherty that follows the struggles of sustenance farmers and fisherman on a windswept island off the western coast of Ireland. Soil for growing potatoes had to be composted from seaweed that islanders hauled up the cliffs in baskets. Prangnell had taught at the Architectural Association in London and was lecturing on architectural theory at Columbia as well as serving as a first-year design critic. Among his more memorable slide lectures were "Man versus Nature," and "Man versus Decor," a treatise on how table settings enhance or inhibit social interchange. Prangnell's studio projects included a summer camp and a motor court, "the oasis," which focused on social interactions with a minimum of architectural interventions. "Peter really stripped away all of our formal preconceptions," recalls Smith. Another influential critic was Giovanni Pasanella whose urban design work with Mayor John Lindsey brought large-scale urban planning into perspective.

Both young architects also shared an interest in historic preservation and lamented the loss of McKim, Mead and White's venerable old Pennsylvania Station. The building was demolished in 1963 but its destruction helped galvanize a concerted preservation movement in America. They attended classes with James Marston Fitch who was lecturing on environmental design and planting the seeds for the first historic preservation program in an American architecture school. They were also attending lectures by the likes of Robert Venturi, Louis Kahn, Paul Rudolph, Jacob Bakema, Herman Hertzberger, Fumihiko Maki, Shadrach Woods and Aldo Van Eyck.

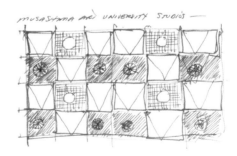

BOTH PAGES:
Travel sketches by
Phillip Smith, Asia, 1972

It was an explosive time to be a student in New York City with so many eye-opening events and exhibitions. Political unrest was brewing on the Columbia campus with anti-war rallies, Students for a Democratic Society (SDS) speeches and sit-ins. In the spring of 1968, demonstrations grew more confrontational as students learned of the university's complicity with the Institute for Defense Analyses (IDA), a weapons think tank linked directly to U.S. involvement in Vietnam. The university was also planning to build what was perceived as a discriminatory gymnasium ("Gym Crow") that encroached on Morningside Park, intruded into the public domain and turned its back on the adjacent Harlem community. Protestors occupied several campus buildings, including Hamilton Hall and Low Library, while the architecture students occupied Avery Hall. All were forcibly removed by riot squads and by early May the entire university had been shut down. Students and faculty from the architecture school restructured the curriculum and design studios to allow for more flexibility. After the first year, students would have more control in their choice of projects and critics. This came to be known as the Platform System which Smith and Thompson would take advantage of when returning to Columbia the next fall.

Meanwhile, Thompson returned to Nantucket for the summer to work on the renovation of a historic house on Broad Street in the main harbor area. He'd spent several summers before on Nantucket studying the island's austere Quaker architecture and the way it accommodated itself to oddly shaped village lots.

At the same time, Smith received a William Kinne Fellows Traveling Fellowship, and traveled overland through Eastern Europe, Turkey, Afghanistan and Iran, arriving in India to study Mughal architecture and visit Balkrishna V. Doshi's studio in Ahmedabad. (Doshi had been a visiting critic at Columbia the year before.) "Doshi's studio was in a built-up urban neighborhood," recalled Smith, "but it had a courtyard, and you went in from this noisy street into a quiet and magic environment." While in India, Smith filled his sketchbooks with drawings of ancient temples, palaces and local domestic architecture as well as modern works such as Le Corbusier's capitol city at Chandigarh and Kahn's Institute of Public Administration in Ahmadabad.

Smith was particularly taken by the way that indigenous Indian buildings were integrated into the natural setting through courtyards, fountains and shaded groves to create sensual environments in opposition to the cold and corporate modernism that prevailed in America and Europe. Later that summer, Smith along with three other Columbia students, organized an international planning workshop in Urbino, Italy with Giancarlo de Carlo, a member of Team X and master planner for the Marchi. This workshop fostered interdisciplinary exchanges between architects and urban planners.

Returning to New York in the fall of 1969, Smith and Thompson began to collaborate on a combined design studio project about Times Square.

OPPOSITE, ABOVE:
Students' Hostel, Ahmedabad, India, Balikrishna Doshi, 1968

OPPOSITE, BELOW:
Gandhi Smarak Sangrahalay, Ahmedabad, India, Charles Correa, 1963

ABOVE:
Indian Institute of Management, Ahmedabad, India, Louis Kahn, 1968

RIGHT:
Travel sketches of Gandhi Smarak Sangrahalay, Phillip Smith

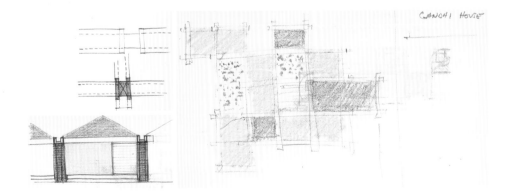

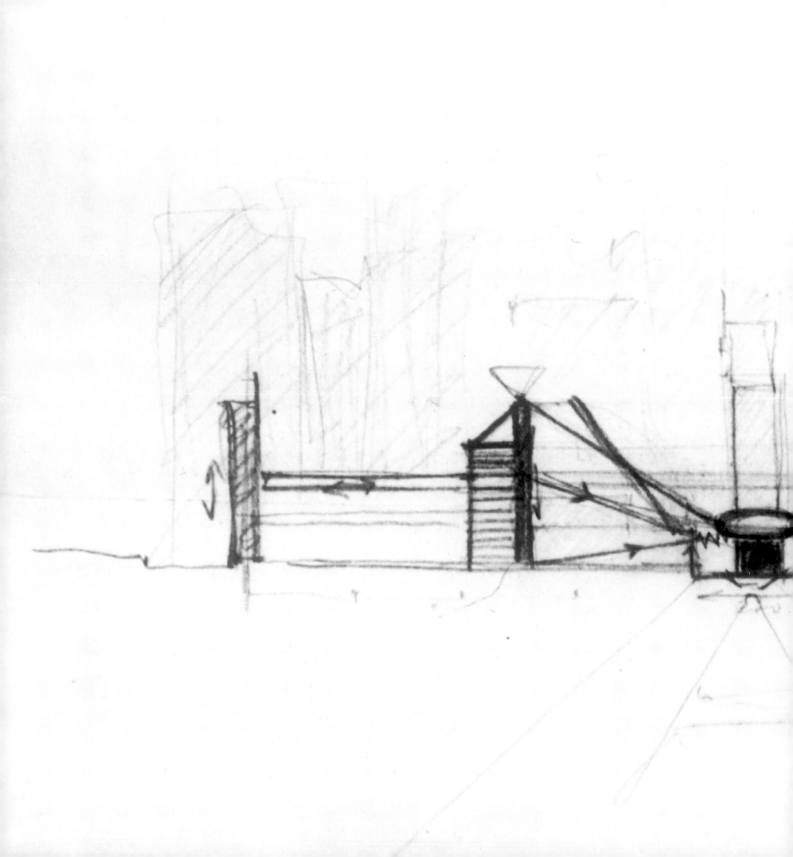

SKY TRANSIT THRU TS?

Times Square: America's greatest outdoor living room
— a contemporary vernacular for decades
— adjusting, growing, disappearing

— the dilemma of how to effect
  universal change in "life patterns" ---

PAGES 24-25:
Section of Times Square with suspended theater, student project, Smith, 1969

LEFT, BELOW:
Kapadvaj, Ghat, India

OPPOSITE, ABOVE:
Section of hotel ,Times Square North, student project, Thompson, 1969

OPPOSITE, BELOW:
Plan of suspended theater over Times Square

PAGES 28-29, LEFT TO RIGHT:
Times Square model with suspended theater and hotel

Model of Times Square Hotel

Theaters, 50th and Broadway, student project, Smith

"There was an effort to clean everything up and gentrify Times Square, but we were trying to be nonjudgmental," says Thompson. "We hoped to make it more pluralistic, even anarchic." The challenge, as they saw it, was to regenerate an increasingly destitute urban landscape by investigating new zoning ordinances and creating accessible mixed-use spaces that combined public and private functions while retaining the eclecticism that made Times Square such a vibrant place to begin with. "We wanted to make it viable but retain excitement and vitality," said the architects who took their investigations into the street and interviewed everyone from developers to homeless people in an attempt to understand the programmatic complexities of different user groups, including neighborhood prostitutes whose insights into territoriality were highly revealing.

Smith and Thompson's thesis was presented as an interdisciplinary project to study the changing nature of the Times Square neighborhood. They worked in collaboration with Fred Pappart of the 42nd Street Development Corporation, students from Columbia's law and business schools as well as the anthropology, psychology and sociology departments. Their plan called for two theaters in the base of a fifty-story

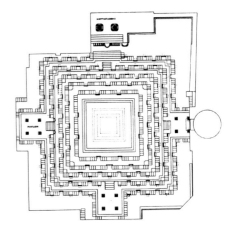

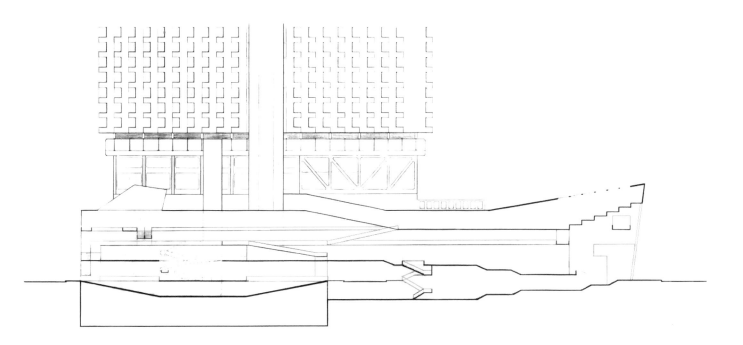

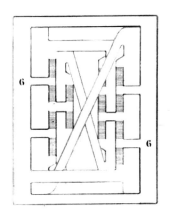

office building, a hotel complex which acted as a "bridge" to Times Square from the north and an elongated concourse that traversed several blocks with a transportation interchange, a museum, restaurants and retail shops. Part of the plan called for a "Sky Transit" and a pendant-like multimedia complex to be suspended from cables over Times Square like an alien pod and filled with a barrage of lightshows, bright signage and interactive arcades. It was a case of McLuhan-meets-Rudofsky-meets-Team X: the gritty and profane intermixed with new typologies and accidental cross-fertilizations.

During the summer of 1970, Thompson also received a Kinne travel grant to study in Japan where among other discoveries he learned about the complex layering of the Shinjuku neighborhood in Tokyo and saw firsthand the rich opportunities of mixing residential and commercial functions. On his way home, he traveled through Southeast Asia and India. After finishing Columbia in 1969, a year earlier than Thompson, Smith would also visit Japan on a six-month fellowship and end up staying and working at Fumihiko Maki's studio in Tokyo. He also worked in Penang, Malaysia with Lim Chong Keat, a founding member of Architects Team Three, but it was Maki who made the deepest impression through his theoretical writings, Group Form, and analysis of soft versus hard space.

TIMES SQUARE "LOBBY" SYSTEM

CASSER TOURS

TIMES GALLERY HOTEL

TS
ST

0   50

25

1 SHOPS
2 RESTAURANT
3 LOBBY
4 DANCE TERRACE
5 KITCHEN
6 BALLROOM
7 STAGE
8 GYM
9 POOL

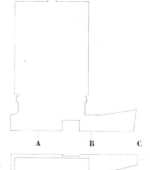

A   B   C

D

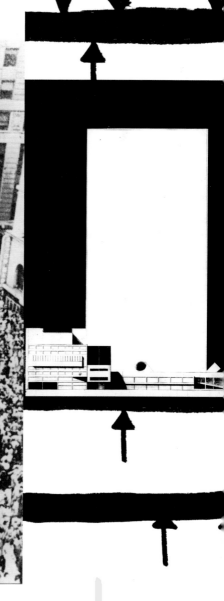

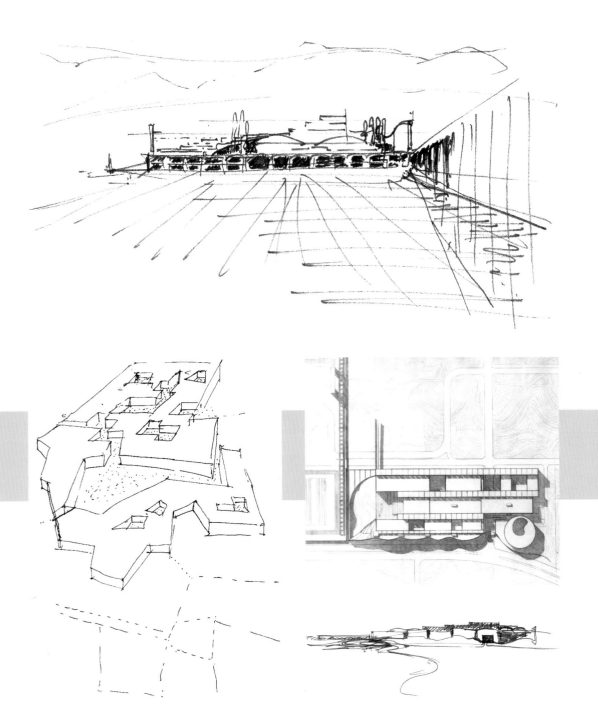

Smith returned to New York in 1974 and worked in the office of William Perrera while Thompson worked for the New York City Planning Commission and the Urban Design Group. In 1975 they moved in together and began working as a team from their apartment on Cathedral Parkway. It was a period of economic recession and there was little work for young architects in New York. Extending some of the ideas they'd explored in their Times Square thesis, they submitted plans for a series of urban competitions including housing for Roosevelt Island, a New Town plan for the Philippines, and a library in Teheran.

The two-phase competition for Roosevelt Island was organized by the New York State Urban Development Corporation to create 1,000 units of high-density housing on a 8.8-acre site in the "Northtown" section. Formerly known as Welfare Island, Roosevelt is a narrow sliver of land that lies in the East River between Manhattan and the borough of Queens. "Behavioral issues in housing design such as child supervision, security, community, and livability will assume equal importance to the formal architectural and the urban design aspects of the solution," read the brief that called for a master plan to accommodate a broad range of income groups and family types. Following the pattern of pre-existing housing blocks designed by José Luis Sert, Smith and Thompson created a sequence of four townhouse blocks, terraced and broken up into discrete entities and

OPPOSITE:
**Site Plan and sketches of
Pahlavi Library competition,
1977**

ABOVE, RIGHT:
**Model and sketch for
Roosevelt Island Competition,
New York City, 1975**

PAGE 33:
**Rendering of Phillipines
Housing Competition, 1975**

separated by green courtyards. These were to have been built along river frontage, looking across to Manhattan while maintaining a strong street facade on the island's main thoroughfare.

Another competition from this period was for the Pahlavi Library in Teheran, Iran (1978.) Smith and Thompson created a "programmed oasis" around which the main functions of the library would be centered. Historical antecedents for this project came from Middle-Eastern bazaars and mosques. To the east, the library was to be enclosed by an undulating, fortress-like band of administrative and service blocks. This facade culminated in a circular chancellery with its own courtyard. Book stacks were contained within a central spine that bisected the complex and provided a circulatory armature for a series of open-air courtyards and public spaces. Environmental design considerations included passive solar orientation, canopies and heat-sink walls. All of the glazed reading rooms and administrative offices were gathered around courtyards that were covered with adjustable sunscreens.

The Philippines competition was part of the "International Design Competition for the Urban Environment of Developing Countries," a program conceived by the staff of *Architectural Record* in 1973 to encourage thoughtful prototypical designs for Third World housing and community development. Smith and Thompson created a flexible template based on traditional kampong housing. They proposed a consistent urban vocabulary to replace a squalid community of pre-existing squatter shacks in Dagat-Dagatan, a reclaimed industrial area to the north of Manila. Each resident was to be given a small plot and the means to build their own house using plywood, steel cables, Philippine mahogany and rattan. Each unit would be raised off of the ground to protect it from monsoon flooding. Walls could be lifted for ventilation while roofs were curved upwards to catch and divert rainwater into a cistern in the Silong, the ground floor space beneath traditional southeast Asian houses. The new Dagat-Dagatan community would be interconnected by a network of footpaths and waterways. (The jury for the competition included Maki and Charles Correa from India.)

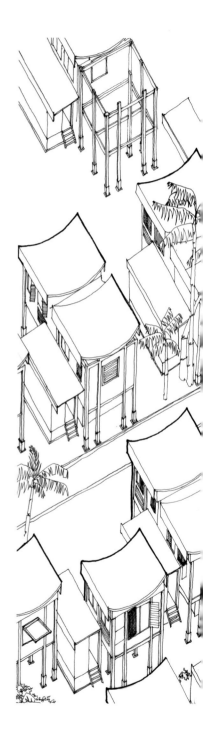

Surfside, Nantucket
Phillip Smith

Smith and Thompson moved to Nantucket for the rest of the year to work on their first built commission: a renovation for Andrew Shunney, an artist and friend who wanted to convert his 18th-century barn into a studio and guesthouse. During their stay on the island, the architects immersed themselves in old Nantucket culture and learned to merge modernist ideas with the local vernacular of shingle walls, brick chimneys, porches and overhanging roofs while working within the guidelines of Nantucket's Historic District Commission, one of the earliest historic districts in the country. They were particularly inspired by Robert Venturi's Trubek and Wislocki houses, built two years earlier on a nearby beach, and how Venturi celebrated New England historicism while still expressing the spatial needs of a modern American lifestyle.

For the Shunney guesthouse and studio, Smith and Thompson expanded the rear of a barn, installed a fireplace and small kitchen and created a sleeping loft opposite a 16-foot-long clerestory window. Though modest in scale, the project was a success and brought the architects additional commissions on Nantucket including a speculative renovation on Howard Street to transform a pre-existing garage and one-story cottage

ABOVE:
**Sketch of Surfside,
Nantucket, Phillip Smith, 1975**

OPPOSITE, MIDDLE:
**Trubek and Wislock houses,
Venturi and Scott Brown,
Polpis, Nantucket, 1970**

OPPOSITE, BELOW:
**Howard Street project,
Nantucket, 1975**

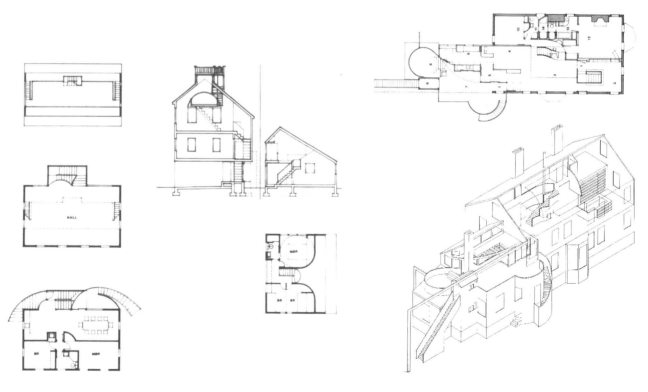

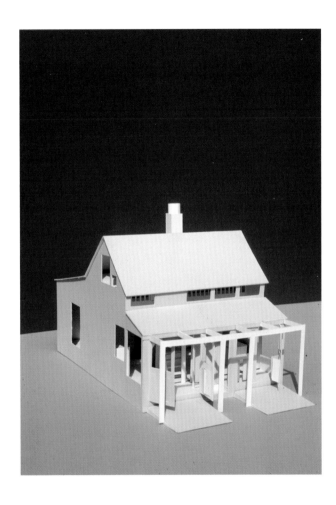

into an integrated living environment. The masonry garage became a kind of *porte-cochère* with an entry court and new staircases at the rear of the building while a third floor was added for views of Nantucket Harbor.

The Webster house, a Federal-style residence, was remodeled with long, drawn out additions that gave it a sense of unity and clarity of circulation. The house was divided into two vertical zones for an extended family: the elder Websters to live on the first floor and the younger generation on the second and third floors. A secret, movable bookcase provided an internal connection between the two families. Smith and Thompson made additions and cuts into the pre-existing structure, opening and exposing parts of the framework, respecting traditional hierarchies while establishing a

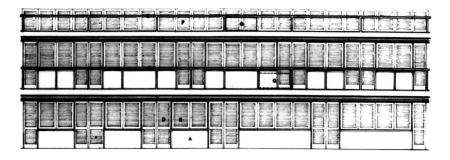

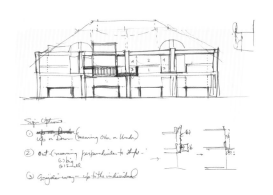

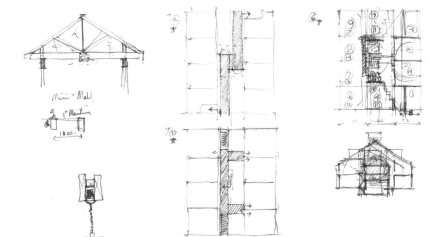

THIS PAGE:
**Sketches and model of
Nantucket Galleria, 1976**

OPPOSITE, ABOVE:
Cut away model for Galleria

OPPOSITE, BELOW:
**Galleria site, former livery
stable on Steamboat Wharf,
Nantucket**

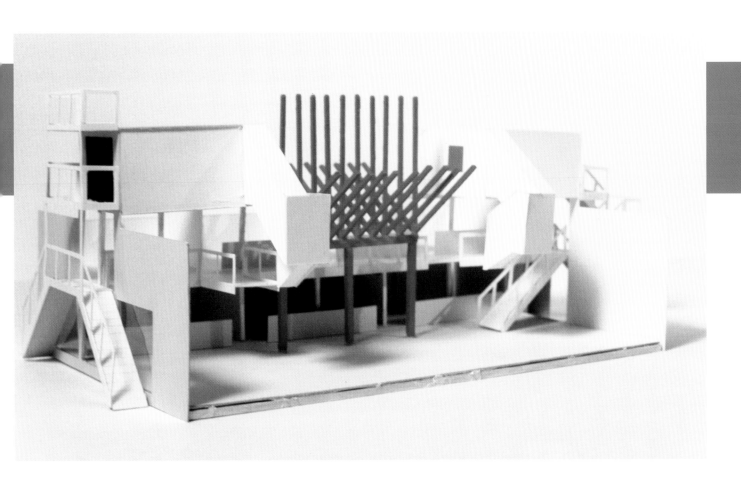

more fluid and modern sequence of interior spaces, including a staggered kitchen and a loft-like, barrel-vaulted studio beneath the upper gable. A curving terrace and pergola were added to the back of the house as well as a semi-enclosed stairway.

For a Boston developer they turned an 1890's livery stable on Steamboat Wharf into a two-level shopping arcade called the Nantucket Galleria (1976). The old structure was renovated to decrease the structural spans of the rafters and to provide extra headroom for sixteen retail units. A boat-shaped skylight in the center of the roof filtered light throughout the interior spaces. "The main facade of the new structure acts as a billboard for the Galleria," wrote Smith and Thompson, "while receiving and discharging customers via two prominent staircases and a two-tiered central portal, allowing for continual circumnavigation throughout the two-story gallery."

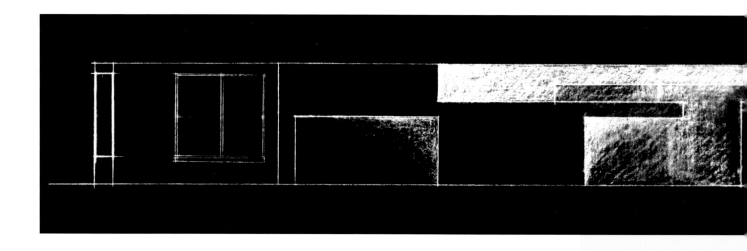

Returning to New York in 1976, Smith and Thompson began work on a series of loft and apartment/townhouse conversions.[3] The majority of their work during the next few years was for a younger generation of urban pioneers, artists, photographers and entrepreneurs who were creating new kinds of lifestyles in old factory buildings and warehouses. This can be seen as the second wave of loft gentrification, a further domestication of the 19th-century sweatshops that flourished in Soho, Tribeca and Chelsea neighborhoods. The first wave, in the 1960s and early 1970s, was characterized by artists inhabiting cheap work/live spaces with minimal changes made to pre-existing structures. Smith and Thompson's projects of the late 1970s and early 1980s signaled a more permanent and established melding into the urban fabric. Many of their clients owned the lofts in question and were willing to commit considerable expense and effort into restoration, remodeling and maintenance--treating their properties as long-term investments rather than temporary, ad-hoc solutions.

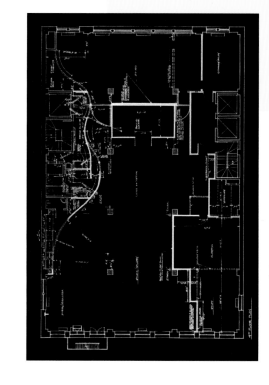

Smith and Thompson devised a kind of "theater of living" for this next generation of urban homesteaders who were inventing multi-purpose environments in which work, family and leisure were combined into a single nonhierarchical space. Every effort was made to preserve the essential rawness of industrial features--concrete coffered ceilings, steel casement windows, columns, beams, etc.--while inserting an edgy sense of drama and further dematerializing box-like uniformity with free standing architectural follies.

ABOVE:
Elevation study for Ross Loft

OPPOSITE, BELOW:
Plan of Ross Loft,
New York City, 1976

RIGHT:
Scholz Penthouse,
New York City, 1978

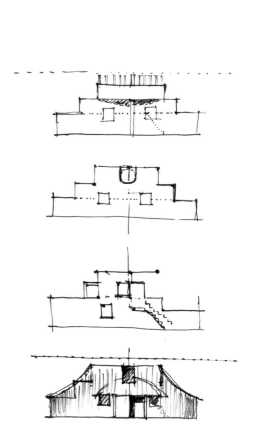

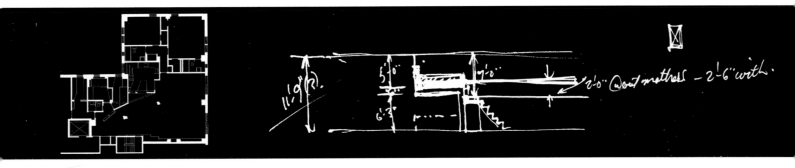

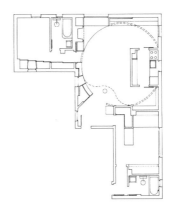

ACROSS:
Studies for Ross nursery and plan of Rudick Apartment, New York City, 1984

OPPOSITE, LEFT:
Ross Loft

OPPOSITE, RIGHT:
Studies for nursery addition of Ross Loft, 1981

ABOVE:
Plan of Scholz Penthouse

PAGE 44-45:
Rudick Apartment

"Blinds" and partitions, often sculptural in nature, were planted around the periphery of the spaces thus allowing the central areas to remain open and free flowing. Most lofts only had windows at the front or back so it was imperative to draw natural light inward toward the deeper recesses of the living and working areas.

Smith and Thompson began work on the Ross loft in 1976. The old factory floors were sanded down and an undulating white wall was built to help animate one side of the long space. The reflective surface of the Alvar-Aalto-inspired wall drew light in from the high, street-side windows and helped to disrupt the uniformity of the old industrial space while also establishing a new zone, concealing utilities and storage areas. Later, when the clients had their first child, the architects added a nursery that was hidden behind a semicircular wall with small, window-like cutouts. The architects' intent was to create a protective enclosure for the newborn child as well as a counterfoil to the drifting expanse of interior space.

Their next residential project was at the opposite end of the economic spectrum: the remodel of a pre-existing penthouse on Park Avenue for Janos Scholz, a rare book collector and renowned cellist (1977.) It was a jumble of cut-up spaces, narrow corridors, and varying ceiling heights. Smith and Thompson adapted some of the same ideas they were using in their lower-budget commissions but on a more sophisticated level. They broke down constricting walls and opened the L-shaped apartment so it felt more like a loft by rounding out corners and elevating the ceiling with a curving, kidney-shaped

recess. Again, the influence of Aalto can be felt. The main space, at the corner, was turned into a rare book library with highly finished maple bookshelves built along the walls and a fireplace set into an inviting corner nook. A tubular white column supports the ceiling and conceals service elements while defining the entry vestibule. The master bedroom lies at the opposite end of the apartment, behind the fireplace wall.

For Pat Rudick, a children's speech therapist, they designed an apartment at 86th Street and Madison Avenue (1984.) As with Scholz, they removed the partitions of a conventional layout and created a large, central living area that made the apartment feel more spacious than it really was. Eccentrically-shaped columns concealed structural and mechanical elements, having the sculptural presence of household gods, while a diagonal, stepped-back wall created trapezoidal complexity. The opposite side of the room featured a 70-foot-long wall of cabinetry made from ash panels with black, tatami-shaped trim that created the mellow feeling of a Japanese teahouse.

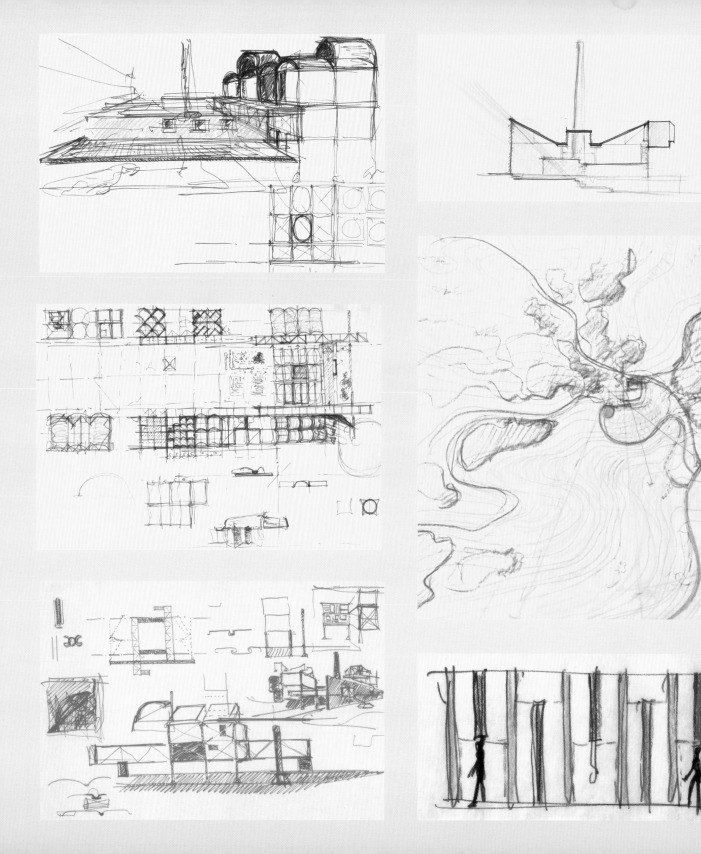

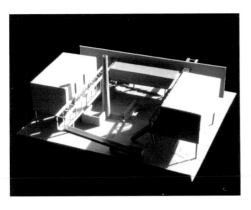

In 1978, Smith and Thompson began the gradual design of an innovative family compound near the Blackwater River in West Virginia, something like a free-form factory with a suspended, truss-style structure. The towering masonry chimney evoked anti-bellum ruins left standing after a wood-framed mansion burned down and it became a landmark in the rolling landscape. To save costs, building components were prefabricated in a modular, four-foot-by-eight-foot grid, and trucked to the isolated location. Living areas were zoned separately for each family and designed to be assembled on site. The master plan also called for a common library and storage locker as well as a common hearth and living terrace to be paved with stone excavated from the rocky site. The swimming pool was fashioned from a dammed-up stream and the communal hearth was housed within a tent-like enclosure with portable screens whenever the compound was in use.

During this same period, Smith and Thompson designed an addition to an existing 1920's country cottage for Sandra Payson that sat on a hillside overlooking Love Lake in Saratoga, N.Y. The remodeled cottage was to be used during the horse-racing season for large events and as a getaway lodge in winter. The client requested the reorganization of the old floor plan and an addition that would engage the lakeside setting while offering a more relaxed and casual style of living. Old Adirondack camps and Japanese ryokans were the prevailing influences on their design. Aside from opening up the interior, the architects expanded the guest rooms while adding a master bedroom suite and a multi-purpose "lake room" that cascaded down the hillside from the main residence.

BOTH PAGES:
**Sketches and model of
Family Compound,
Blackwater, WV, 1978**

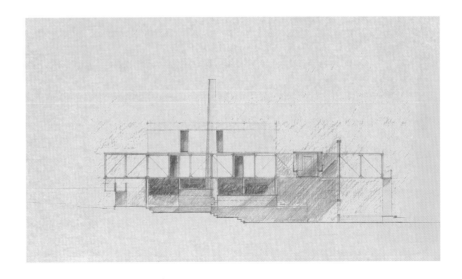

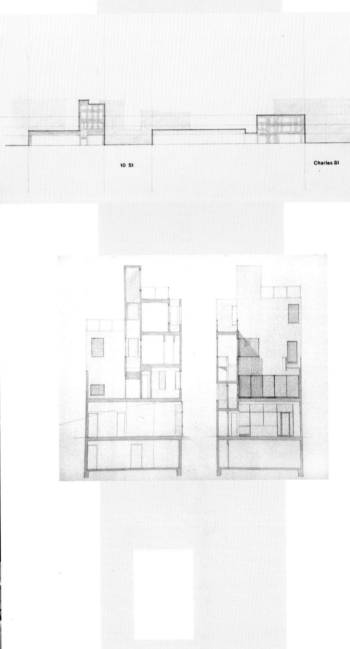

48

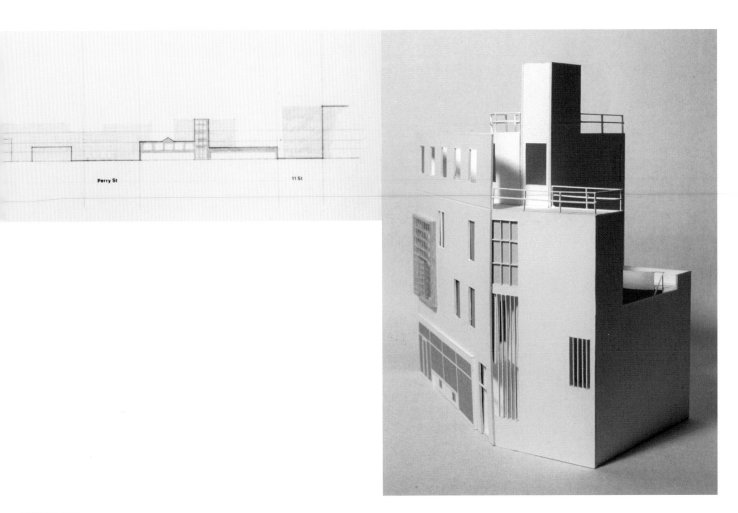

OPPOSITE, LEFT:
Traditional Wind tower,
Bandar Abbas, Iran

ABOVE, RIGHT:
Sketches and model
of Colglazier building,
Greenwich Village,
New York City, 1981

PAGE 50:
Colglazier building

PAGE 51:
Interior of "wind tower",
plans and facade study of
Colglazier building

In 1981, Smith and Thompson began work on their first from-the-ground-up structure, a mixed-use building on Seventh Avenue, for Duane Colglazier, a former Wall Street trader who owned the Pleasure Chest, a well-known adult boutique. Colglazier had purchased an 831-square-foot lot between Charles and Perry Streets and worked with the architects to develop a "village type" rhythm of different structures behind a single wall of brick that followed the line of Seventh Avenue, helping to unify all the parts. An Arabic style bay window was fabricated from a grid of Purpleheart wood to screen and to shade the residential interior like a veil and create a sense of mystery. The facade along Seventh Avenue echoed the scale and fenestration of the Greenwich Village Historical District.

Perry St   11 St

New York City Zoning allowed only a single story commercial space with a small one level apartment above, but the architects found a way to work with the Board of Standards and Appeals to create a three-story townhouse with a maximum allowable floor area and a roof terrace above the commercial space. A rear courtyard provided the required open space at the second level.

In a relatively small building, Smith and Thompson managed to combine a number of fairly complex moves including a false-front brick facade rising an extra story without adding to the limited legal floor area. The wall is penetrated by five window-like openings and narrow staircase tower rises above the fourth floor.

While modernist in form and surface, the building conveys a vernacular interweaving of discrete spaces and connections as if they'd accrued naturally over time. For inspiration, Smith and Thompson were also looking at plans of 18th-century Parisian hotels that echoed the acute angles of intersecting avenues. They were also making explicit reference to a house and wind tower that Smith had seen while visiting Bandar Abbas, Iran in 1968. A narrow structure rose several stories to scoop the breezes coming off the Persian Gulf and cooled the interior of the dwelling. The Colglazier project proved to be a major step forward for the firm, moving them beyond the loft/apartment genre towards a more complex urban narrative.

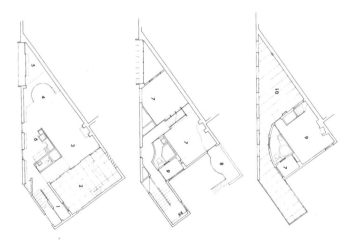

NARRATIVES OF BUILDING

During the 1980s, Smith and Thompson began to work in the Hamptons, on eastern Long Island, and fell under the spell of the sea-reflected light and the natural beauty of the low-lying landscape that had, over the years, influenced so many poets, artists and architects before them. The region possesses a rich legacy of experimentation from Jackson Pollock and Robert Motherwell to architects like Peter Blake, Andrew Geller, Charles Gwathmey and Norman Jaffe. There are architectural icons that would rank high on any stage such as Pierre Chareau's house/studio for Motherwell in East Hampton, Blake's Pinwheel House in Water Mill, Geller's Pearlroth House in Westhampton Beach, Gwathmey's house and studio for his parents in Amagansett, Richard Meier's Saltzman House in East Hampton and Jaffe's integrated arrangement of earth-hugging residences at Sam's Creek, Bridgehampton.[4] The bar was set high for younger architects who ventured out and had to live up to such lofty examples, or at the very least, acknowledge their precedence.

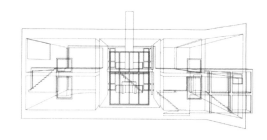

There were also important residential projects by Robert Venturi, Robert Stern and Jaquelin Robertson that flirted on the edges of historicism and, in turn, inspired a wave of postmodern pastiche and historic appropriation. By the mid-1980s, neo-Shingle-Style cottages and faux-Palladian villas were sprouting along the dunes and potato fields of the Hamptons generating a fashionable pressure to conform.

"Despite this trend we were exhilarated by the possibilities of building in such a setting," said Smith. Their work from this period breathes in the sea and salt air, opens up, combines materials, forms and, in a sense, coalesces into a hybrid of old and new, eastern and western themes that became recognizable as their own signature brand,

PAGES 52-53:
Concept sketch of East Hampton Airport

ABOVE, LEFT:
Hook Pond, East Hampton, New York

ABOVE:
Perspective of Kleeb Residence, East Hampton, New York, 1987

OPPOSITE, UPPER LEFT:
Phillip Smith at Kleeb Residence

OPPOSITE, UPPER RIGHT:
Model of Kleeb Residence

OPPOSITE, BELOW:
Kleeb Residence

54

55

ROOM ON THE ROOF

Robert Kleeb's approach to weekend relaxation is a party on the rooftop deck of his Long Island home

ARCHITECTURE
OF THE PARTY

In the Hamptons, almost every home has an outdoor porch. But not many are as creatively placed as the rooftop deck incorporated by architects G. Phillip Smith and Douglas Thompson into their plan for the Kleeb residence. What makes it work?

1. A shelved nook in the roof pavilion's outer wall not only shelters the buffet, but also houses outdoor speakers, lighting and firewood storage.

2. Lookout bench has a back-rest that flips to take advantage of bay- or seaward views.

3. Pressure-treated decking is arranged in 3'x4' squares, which can be lifted up for roof access.

4. A bulky kitchen vent is hidden in the base of the stationary cedar table.

BOTH PAGES:
Kleeb Residence featured in Home Magazine, 1989

following the trajectory of earlier academic and professional explorations. They combined a modernist aesthetic of open transparent plans and geometrically pure forms with vernacular textures and traditions, this without bending too far towards historical replication.

In 1983 Robert Kleeb asked them to design a weekend house in Wainscott Hills on one of the highest points in the Hamptons. The property was not far from the East Hampton Airport and high enough to gain views of the ocean to the south and Northeast Harbor to the north. Kleeb, an executive with Mobile Oil, met Smith while working in Singapore in the early 1970s. He was unswayed by the trend of neo-traditional architecture and gave the architects a free hand in every aspect of the design development. While the house ended up being emphatically contemporary, it was sympathetic to the vacation vernacular of the region.

"It's really a compact form with cut-outs and a circulation spine that stretches out to engage the landscape," said Thompson, explaining how the Kleeb House was strategically sited to catch prevailing southwesterly winds. It was only one room deep, similar to 19th-century summer cottages, with terraces outside of each room. A vertical order grew around the armature of the fireplace rising through the center of the house. Cedar shingles clad exterior walls and helped define cubic volumes and create surface tension. The whiteness and smoothness of certain walls, trim, railings and outrigger beams stood in contrast to weathered shingled surfaces and created compositional complexity. It was a treatment that suggested New England traditions without resorting to slavish duplication. Native blueberry bushes and black pines were planted to further blend the architecture of the house into the rolling, scrubby landscape.

While being a relatively small weekend house at 2,500 square feet, there were numerous effects that made it appear larger and more complex than it really was. Just as they'd orchestrated a sequence of living stations in their Manhattan lofts, Smith and Thompson brought a sense of verticality to the pastoral setting of the Hamptons. An elongated white wall acted as a kind of horizontal spine that reached into the landscape and anchored the house to its site, punctuated as it was by a series of openings that acted as framing devices. Living areas expanded and mounted up like building blocks, stacked and interspersed with sun decks, terraces, and walkways, set back in diminishing sizes, all the way up to a small pavilion and roof deck. The various levels rose like mesas from the lower-level garage to the main living room, a second floor with bedrooms, a penthouse pavilion and finally, a party deck with a ship's ladder that led up to the rooftop terrace and a modern widow's walk that delivered the ultimate views of ocean and bay. The Kleeb House proved to be a lyrical mediation between urban tension and rural release, a place to interact with nature and to relax without losing touch with the city's dynamic rhythms.

PAGES 58-59:
Kleeb Residence, living room interior and exterior

TOP:
Kleeb Residence, stair to the pool

OPPOSITE:
Kleeb Residence

The Van Zandt House (East Hampton, 1987) can be seen as a continuation and complement to Kleeb, as if they were panels in a single diptych. Both projects were conceived during the same period and within similar landscapes. Both evolved from a kind of hybridized urban/rural conversation and both employed similar types of architectural vocabulary. Pamela Van Zandt, an editor at *Vogue*, had seen renderings of the Kleeb house and admired the interplay of modern versus vernacular so invited the firm to design a weekend house on a three-acre wooded plot on Orchard Road. It was clear from the start that the client had eclectic tastes. She'd already invited proposals by other architects, including Steven Holl, and her house became something like a charrette, a mini competition in contemporary residential design.

Smith and Thompson combined guest facilities and the main house without building separate buildings. The scale of parts and massing echoed the add-on architecture of the area's 18th- and 19th-century cottages. Large areas of glass were broken up by white mullions. A *porte-cochère* passed beneath the "hinge" of the two wings and served to separate the guest area from the private wing. As with Kleeb, there was a sense of

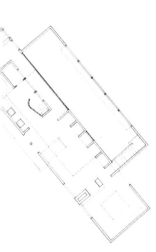

continuity, an accretion of parts. Similarly, the Van Zandt house had a three-story tower that acted as a central spine and gave order to the rest of the building. Pyramidal skylight roofs rose over the master bedroom and gym to bring in natural light and suggest farmhouse ceilings.

"Although geographic constraints ordered open spaces to the north and protected facades to the south, the dual axes of the house are sculpted to provide light and ventilation from the east, west, north and south," wrote Smith and Thompson. "The east and south facades maintain privacy but allow sunlight to penetrate deeply through both wings, protected by shade trees in the summer. The north and west facades provide specific but open views to the garden and woods beyond while allowing additional controlled light into the house through insulated translucent panels."

Both the Van Zandt and Kleeb houses represented a convergence of modern with more rustic themes, as well as a village-like massing and sense of scale that the firm would exploit more fully in future projects.

In 1989, a design competition was announced for a new terminal at the East Hampton Airport and the architects were eager to submit plans. "There were so many interesting possibilities," said Thompson. "The competition addressed all of the issues that we'd been dealing with up to that point." They'd become familiar with the site while working on the Kleeb house whose hilltop site overlooked the airport grounds. The competition called for a new 4,000 square foot terminal to replace a dilapidated structure built in the 1920s. There were a few World War II era hangars, outlying machine shops and storage buildings on a site that was otherwise open and flat, surrounded by low-lying hills and a thick forest of pitch pine and scrub oak.

The first image that came to mind was Le Corbusier's 1946 proposal for an airport as a simple line drawn in a field. "The beauty of an airport is in the splendor of wide open spaces," wrote Corb, who believed that nothing should compete with the mechanical integrity of the airplane itself. Smith and Thompson's initial concept was something like a nomad's tent in the desert that would serve to punctuate the sweeping expanse of land and sky. "We were trying to get as close as possible to the feeling of a pavilion in a field," said Smith.[5] This initial idea evolved into a long and narrow, one story building with a distinctive brise-soleil at its center. Following Corb's thoughts, Smith and Thompson's terminal was hardly there at all, the mere whisker of a profile on the windswept airfield.

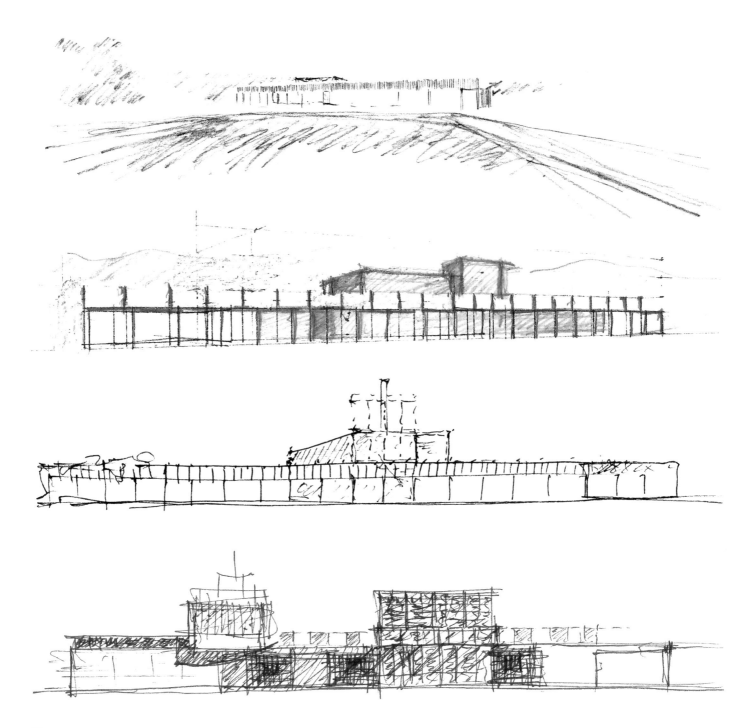

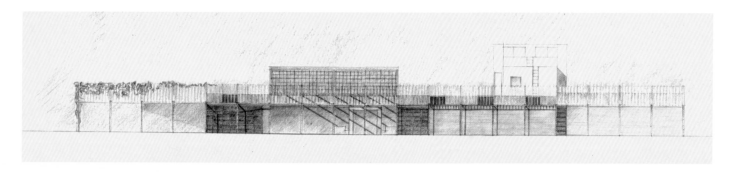

**East Hampton Airport
Competition winning entry
model, East Hampton,
New York, 1989**

OPPOSITE:
**Studies for East Hampton
Airport**

ABOVE:
**Elevation of East Hampton
Airport**

BELOW LEFT:
**Airport sketch, Le Corbusier,
1946**

BELOW RIGHT:
**Mogul encampment
from Bernard Rudofsky,
*'Architecture Without
Architects'***

You could see right through the lobby and out to the airplanes. The landside of the terminal was anchored by a long arbor that ran 200 feet along the entry facade to instill a breezy sense of domestic comfort for departing passengers, evoking as it did traditional garden pergolas and dune fencing.

The tubular steel uprights were to be planted with wisteria or another climbing vine to soften the edges and make the architecture blend into its surroundings. Walls would have been clad with horizontal cedar siding stained driftwood gray while the trellis work and window trim were to be painted a phosphorescent white.

The simple layout was strung out like a train from south to north with a waiting area, snack bar, baggage claim, administration offices and a covered garage for emergency vehicles. A semi-circular tower rose above the airside of the building and provided 180-degree views over the tarmac and runways. Everything was designed to celebrate arrival and departure and to create a recognizable identity from both the air and the ground, one that would be appropriate for an exclusive beach resort like East Hampton.

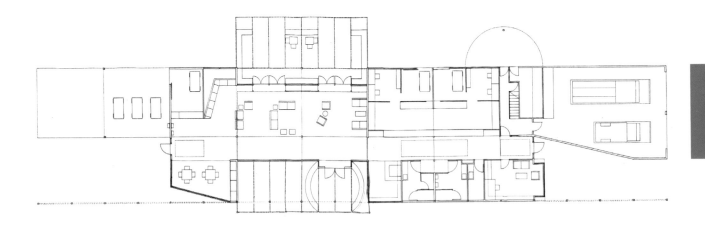

ABOVE AND OPPOSITE ABOVE:
Plan, renderings and model
for East Hampton Airport

BELOW:
Competition team with design
boards for East Hampton
Airport

OPPOSITE, LOWER LEFT:
Isometric study of entrance
arbor

PAGES 70-71:
Model of the airport terminal
developed for the Town of
East Hampton

The jury, which included Charles Gwathmey, William Pedersen and Jordan Gruzen, selected five finalists and when the Town Board met to make the final decision, the Smith and Thompson entry was chosen. The firm refined their scheme, working closely with town and airport authorities, but there was a certain amount of controversy from the start. Indeed, all of the finalist designs were perceived as being too "modernistic" and offensive for the aura of benign entitlement that local politicians and real estate interests felt that the Hamptons should represent. In fact, it brought to a head a bigger argument about "modern" versus "traditional" aesthetics that was very much in the air during that period.

The irony was that Smith and Thompson's hybrid approach--as with Kleeb, Van Zandt and now this understated airport terminal--ran counter to the very type of aggressive design that many people were afraid of. Stories appeared in the *New York Times* and *New York Magazine* that further fueled the debate.[6]

In the end, a November 1989 referendum to fund the new terminal was defeated by a narrow margin.

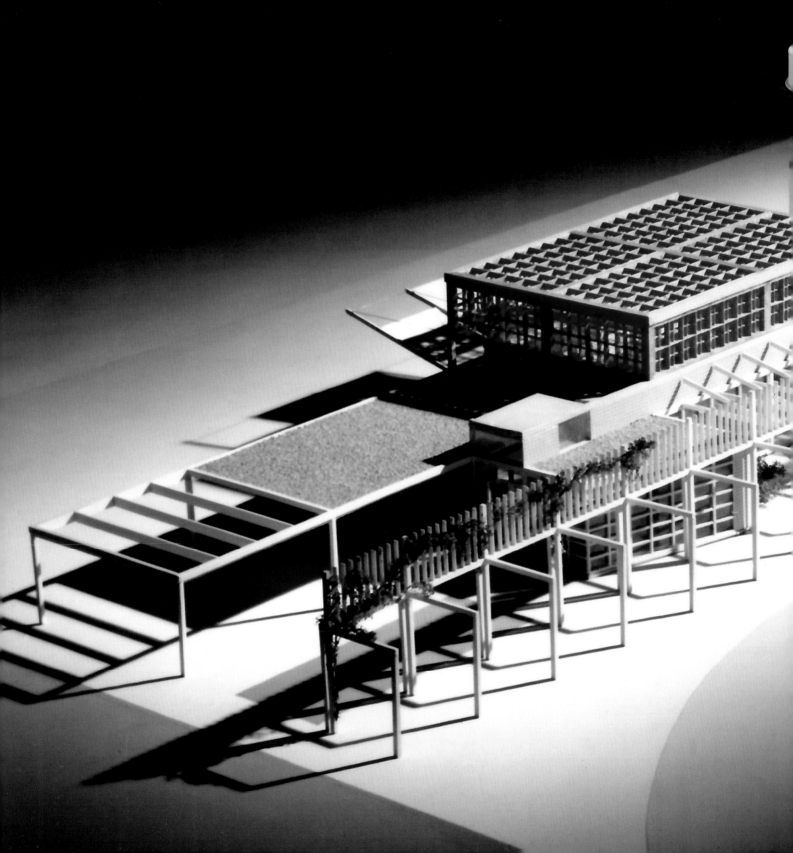

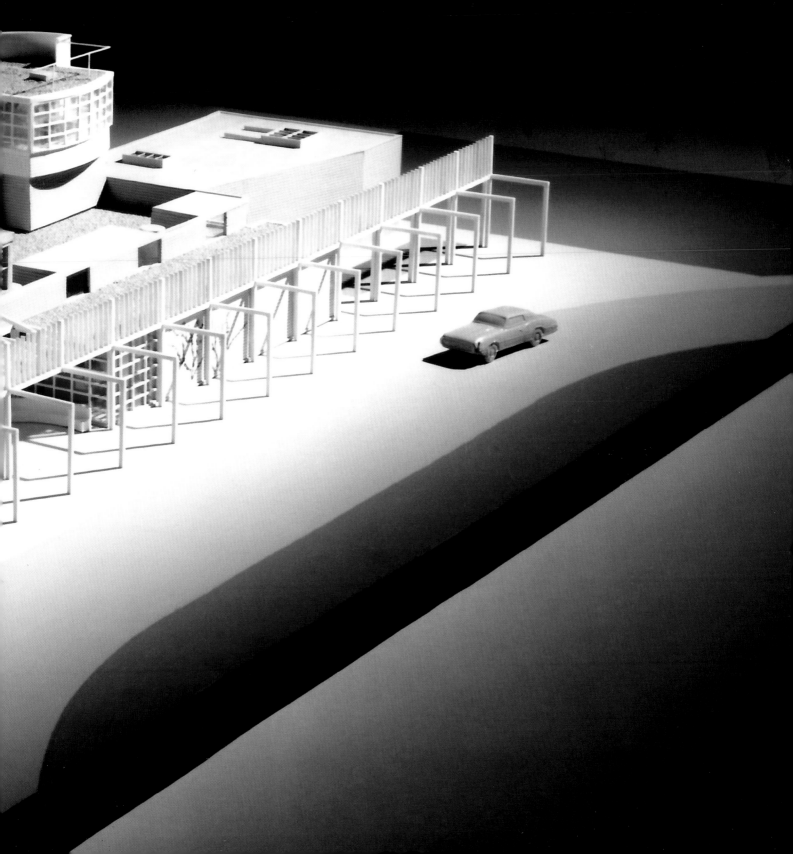

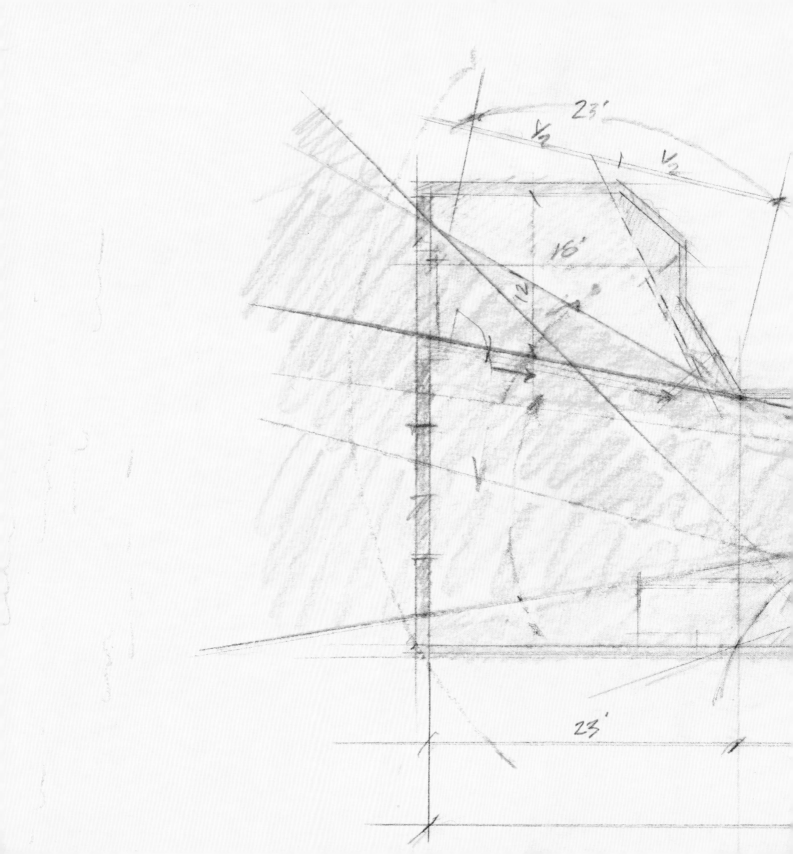

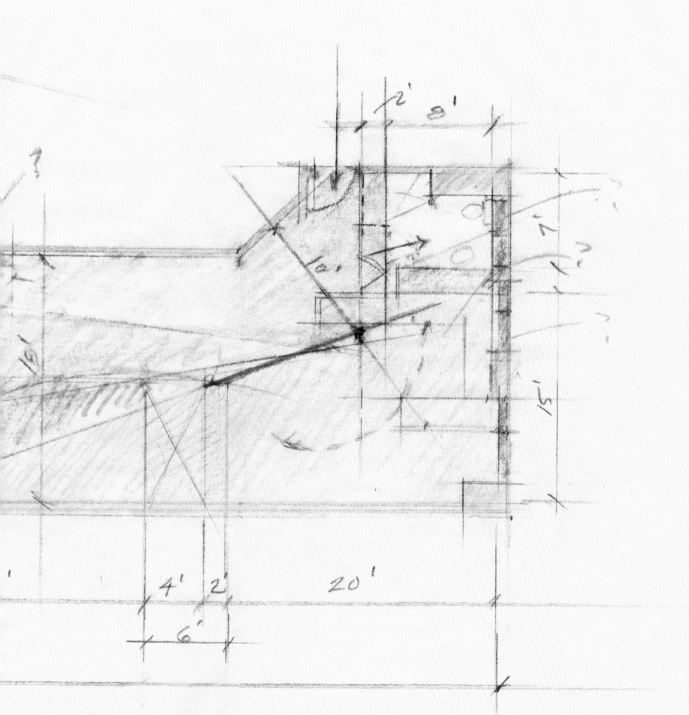

Between the early 1990s and 2000, Smith and Thompson completed a series of residential and non-residential remodels in older industrial and commercial buildings. As with their earlier loft projects, the architects were concerned with vectoring natural light into the deepest, darkest recesses of the buildings in question. The pre-existing structures were seen as temporary shells while the dwelling and/or institutional insertions were designed like migratory nests: modern, rhythmic structures, self-contained and flexible, almost nomadic in nature as if the occupants were only temporary visitors, passing through.

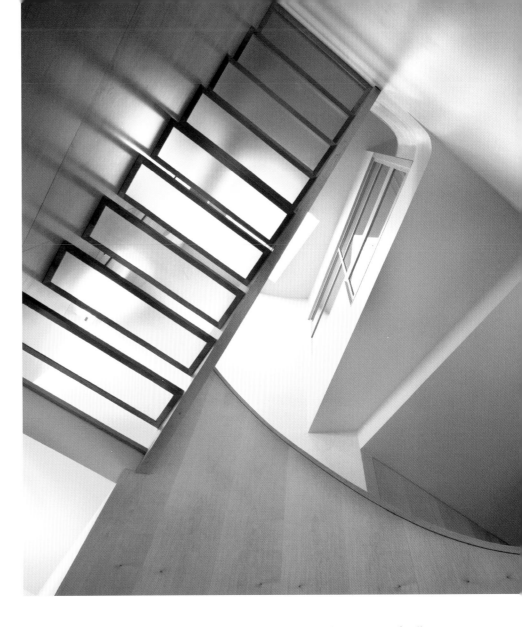

In a study for one of their urban lofts, Smith and Thompson drew a cone of yellow pencil, almost like the beam from a lighthouse or a slide projector, that penetrated all the way to a single point at the back of the loft. Reflective surfaces and free-standing walls were angled to channel and enhance this luminous penetration. [7]

In a loft for Mary and Jonathan Sibley, a thin, ribbon-like railing was made to hover above a maple staircase without any apparent support. It provided a sculptural focal point and connective narrative for a conversion in the top two floors of an industrial

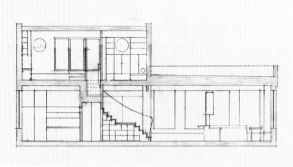

building on Irving Place. The clients, who had lived and worked in Japan, wanted a Zen-like simplicity so the architects created a quiet, ceremonial progression of spaces with pale maple panels. Black detailing offered stark contrast to the white walls and stripped oak flooring. Cabinets and eccentrically-shaped drawers were tucked between walls and beneath the staircase to provide extra storage space. A fireplace was made from steel cubes stacked in diminishing sizes to create a skyscraper-style massing in the main living room, paying homage to the Chrysler and Empire State Buildings that could be seen through two large windows in the same room. An elegant black railing rose and turned with the stairs that led the eye and body up to the mezzanine work level which, in turn, opened out to a north-facing roof terrace.

Maple was also the wood of choice for the Spencer/Booker Loft (1997) designed for an Australian couple who gave frequent fundraising parties for the United Nations and other causes. Their loft on Lafayette Street, north of Houston, was kept as open and multi-functional as possible. Laminated glass panels, sidelights and transom windows

LEFT:
Sibley Loft,
New York City, 1992

UPPER RIGHT:
Study section, Sibley Loft

LOWER RIGHT:
Travel sketch of Japanese
storage steps, Phillip Smith,
1972

OPPOSITE:
Sibley Loft staircase with
storage boxes

PAGE 78, LEFT:
Spencer Loft, open kitchen,
New York City, 1997

PAGE 79, RIGHT:
Spencer Loft, paneled wall

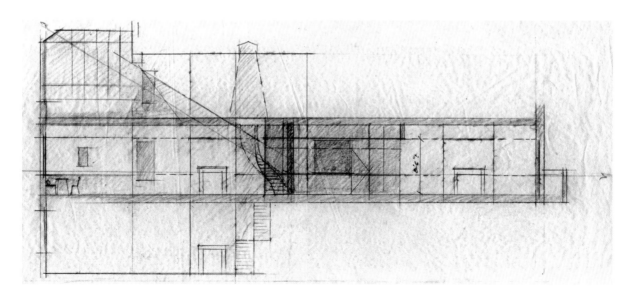

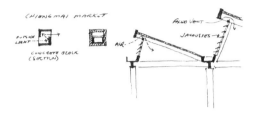

were used to saturate the 1640-square-foot space with natural light which reflected off the white ceiling, pale maple cabinets and wall panels. A collage-like arrangement of storage shelves, drawers, and cabinets ran along the back end of the loft and included a system of folding shutters to screen a large window facing a nearby industrial building.

The De Benedetto/Jiang Loft (2001) was yet another exercise in adapting a long, narrow envelope with sculptural insertions while enhancing views and coaxing light back into deeper cavities. The loft was located on Charlton Street, between Greenwich and Hudson Street, on the third floor of an old industrial building with expansive views over the Hudson River. Maple cabinetry and translucent panels absorbed light and suffused the space with transcendent luminosity. Smith and Thompson created a 40-foot-long diagonal slice of black steel as the dominant gesture that swept from the back of the loft towards the front and the main source of light. It also served as a structural support for lightweight partitions and cabinetry along one side of the loft. Sandblasted plexiglass walls and pivoting panels brought a degree of privacy to the master bedroom without blocking any light. The kitchen/dining area was open and freeform with a smooth concrete countertop and extendable eating surfaces. A guest-and-media room was tucked within a bulging corner and closed off with sliding panels of plexiglass.

Jeffrey Krauss, a venture capitalist and Debby Vilas, a child psychologist, wanted to combine the top three floors of a townhouse that stood directly behind the Guggenheim Museum, on the Upper East Side. As with all of Smith and Thompson's urban projects, channeling light was the major design objective. A dramatic staircase with glass treads rose beneath a large skylight so that light could penetrate all three levels of the townhouse. The light-absorbing staircase became the crystalline heart of the project. Its shaft was clad in light maple paneling to further reflect light into the lower recesses where it wrapped around a guest bathroom with a frosted-glass ceiling.

In an effort to break the claustrophobic conditions of the conventional office cubicle, Smith and Thompson created a "paralegal village" for the National Realty company at 280 Park Avenue with alcoves in the shape of trapezoidal "hives" that suggested Bedouin tents or teepees. The sloping walls and slat windows of these structures added a syncopated rhythm to the otherwise static interior, humanizing and animating the predictable monotony of the work environment. Each hive was given a unique shape to help office workers identify their respective spaces. Each had open ceilings to bring in more light and stained glass windows to personalize and further distinguish one from the other. Mobile workstations occupied the central space while alcoves with fixed

partitions ran around the outer walls. The space-demanding law library was dismantled and rebuilt around the perimeter. All new insertions were prefabricated in maple by a cabinetmaker in Brooklyn and installed over a long weekend, thus preventing any downtime for the office.

The Caravan Institute was a non-profit organization founded in 1929 to further education and the arts. It was also the largest Italian language school in New York City. The challenge for Smith and Thompson was to reorganize the circulation of the existing building--a faux medieval structure on East 65th Street off Lexington Avenue--and create a "community" for learning by adding four new classrooms as well as rationalizing the circulation and the arrangement of common spaces. The idea was to create a looser, less formal hierarchy of spaces within a relatively rigid, pre-existing layout. The architects were inspired, fittingly, by the work of Italian architect Carlo Scarpa in the way he combined arcane methodologies with modern resources and mysteriously hidden sources of light.

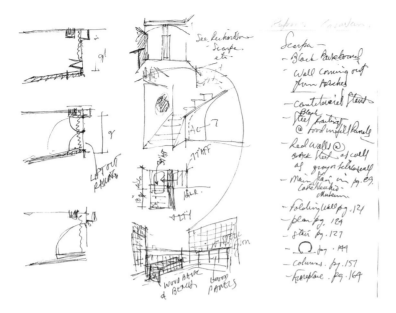

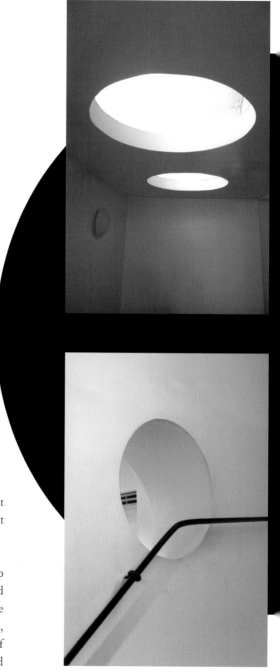

Starkly sculptural details were used in many of the doorways and railings, a kind of architectural calligraphy that signaled movement and intuitive circulation, in contrast to the blank walls, restored wood floors and ceilings of the original interior. The first level had an administrative office, reception area and two classrooms in the rear. From the narrow entry point, the eye was led down the length of a gallery to a single column, stained black, and beyond to a new Italian travertine stairway and classrooms. The wall behind the reception desk featured an oculus-type opening that allowed a seductive glimpse of what was otherwise concealed: a staircase with black steel railing, similar to the one in the Sibley Loft, that led up to the second floor and another series of classrooms. The first classroom, at the top of the stairs, was enclosed within a curving plaster rotunda that had small, punched-out windows and a narrow clerestory.

Smith and Thompson's brief for the Youthstream Media Company (2000) was to map and navigate a cavernous expanse for a new dot.com company, making it playful and coherent at the same time. The sprawling, 44,000 square foot space, filled the entire second floor of the iconic Chrysler Center, a block-long building on 43rd Street, between Lexington and Third Avenue. The idea was to suggest an ephemeral kind of geography and new frontiers in cyber space. Village-like clusters of workstations and

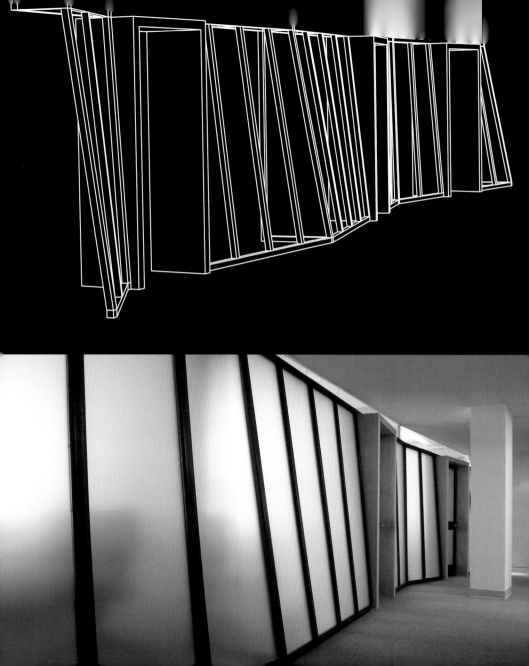

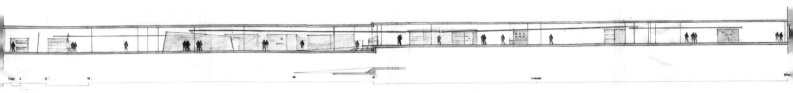

free-form partitions related to various departments--marketing, design, executive--with color-coded walls and flooring to help establish a sense of direction and spatial hierarchy. There was no overall lighting for the general space, but overhead communication tracks were illuminated with light emitting diodes (LEDs,) which created "pathways of light" hanging from the ceiling. Circulation patterns were laid out according to the street grid of Manhattan with the main east-to-west passageway being Broadway (on a slight diagonal), while Park Avenue and 34th Street were long perpendiculars and Times Square was a central meeting, or "vision" area. A digital messaging system ran throughout the space and the main server room hovered within a glass-enclosed cube with a backlit access floor. Youthstream Media was dissolved during construction and the design plans were sold to an advertising company that took over the lease of the space.

PAGES 86-87:
Classroom complex, Caravan Italian Language Institute

OPPOSITE:
Tarragon Realty, W 54th Street, New York City, 2005

ABOVE:
Section of Youthstream Media Offices, Chrysler Center, New York City, 2000

BELOW:
Partial plan of Tarragon Realty, 2005

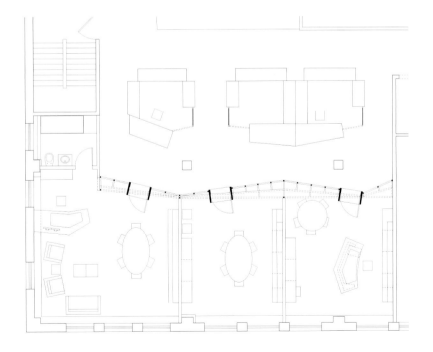

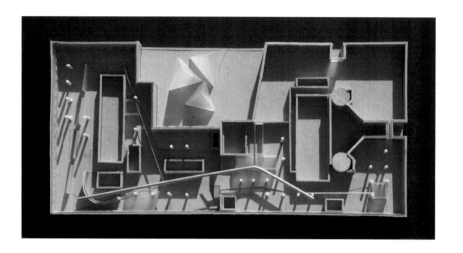

For Tarragon Realty, Smith and Thompson opened up the interior of the historic General Motors building (1909) at Broadway and 57th Street. They raised the ceiling around the perimeter of the main space and introduced translucent plexiglass walls and clear glass doors for the legal offices. Dropped ceilings were removed and all mechanical systems were clustered near the center to allow full-height windows looking north to Central Park, south down Broadway and west to the Hudson River. White walls and maple counters, partitions and cabinets lightened the overall effect.

For Ursus Art Books on 22nd Street between 6th and 7th Avenues, the architects created a public, street-level presence for the mail-order company that specialized in art and architecture books. They tried to keep the space as open as possible with islands for book displays and an alcove with rare books using a mix of standardized shelving and custom-fabricated maple counters and tables. The tall windows in the rear of the store were shielded by pivoting translucent polycarbonate panels. The required security monitors were housed within an entry pavilion and a large, cloud-like chandelier hanging just inside to celebrate entry from the street. Pre-existing structural columns with Doric capitals were enhanced as "pathfinders" with vertical tubes of light, while laser-cut steel signage and window display systems were designed to allow views in and out of the store.

ABOVE:
Youthstream Media offices model, Chrysler Center, 2000

OPPOSITE:
Ursus Books, W 20th Street, New York City, 2000

VACANT LOTS

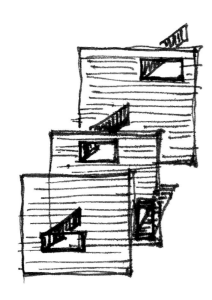

"We have this thing about vacant lots," Doug Thompson said. "It's the blank piece of paper, the empty canvas. We always had a dream to claim a corner of space and build ourselves an oasis in New York." This was the inspiration behind the mixed-use building that they designed with a gallery, and a studio and residence for themselves, on the northwest corner of 10th Avenue at 23rd Street in Manhattan. Long before this opportunity arose, they'd worked out their own personal style of guerilla development that seems quite unique to their practice, beginning with the discovery and reclamation of neglected, leftover urban spaces--an approach they'd first explored in their Times Square thesis at Columbia and would investigate further in small, infill projects.

An idea took seed in 1982 with a combined residential and office commission for Peter G. Davis. This was when they discovered the exciting possibilities of building on Manhattan rooftops. Davis, a music critic, owned the top two floors of a narrow building at 71st Street and West End Avenue. Smith and Thompson created a freestanding pavilion with a barrel vaulted roof set in a rooftop garden with pergola and plantings. "It was important to celebrate being at the top of the building, up in the sky," said Smith. It was to be a listening room and archive for the client's extensive record collection with glass doors and narrow terraces at either end. "It's another village up there," said Smith at the time. "It's different from the rest of the city--more like a Greek hill town--and has its own form and character."

The important lesson the architects learned from this early rooftop exercise was how to infiltrate New York's vertical frontier and retrofit new kinds of urban homesteads into unconventional situations. Smith and Thompson built on this experience and began to experiment with other sites. Their approach derived in part from the hands-on design/ build spirit of the sixties--finding, reclaiming, and otherwise "liberating" property--in a legal, but hardly less inventive way. They learned to stalk vacant properties, absorb the mood and texture of surrounding neighborhoods, study adjacent architecture, work on site, be resourceful, innovative and always patient. They also learned to parse the arcane language of city zoning and building codes, always looking for unforeseen advantages.

Haus-Rucker-Co., a collaborative of Austrian architects who established themselves in the late 60s through radical street actions, published a pamphlet in 1976 called 'Rooftop Oasis Project' that outlined the methods and laws that governed viable rooftop projects in New York City. "If a proposal uses a rooftop as an extension of existing uses already permitted in the building, and the building's use within the zoning district is legal in the first place, there should be no zoning problems." [8] Similarly, whenever the architects came upon a vacant lot, they would fantasize about building something on it. "It's a way for us to form our thoughts and imagine how our input might enhance the existing context," said Smith. They discovered many such lots on weekend excursions around Manhattan, and finally settled on an overgrown parcel of land on Cathedral Parkway, between Broadway and Amsterdam Avenue, one block from the Cathedral Church of St. John the Divine. They'd been scouting the 25-by-70-foot lot since 1976, the year they returned from Nantucket. They called the number on the dilapidated "For Sale" sign only to find that it had been disconnected. (Taxes were paid from an unknown address in New Jersey.) After considerable effort, they managed to contact the owner who agreed to give them a year-long option to purchase the site in exchange for the payment of outstanding property taxes. This would give the architects enough time to develop plans. They extended the option for a second year and, by the end of 1979,

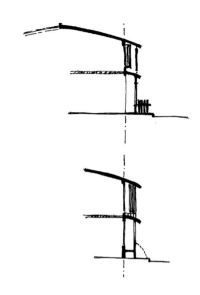

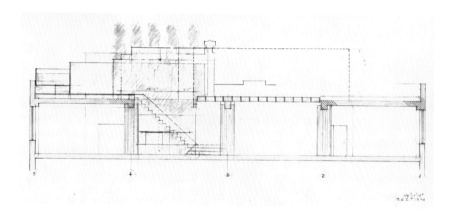

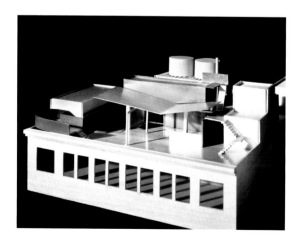

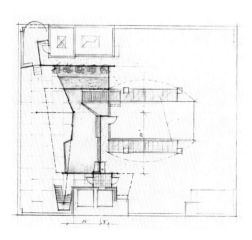

were able to buy the land for a relatively small amount. "We spent every penny we had," recalls Thompson.

A year after completing the Davis project (1982), Smith and Thompson began construction of a freestanding, multi-level building on the Cathedral Parkway site. They conceived of a narrow high-rise with a three bedroom, co-op apartment on every floor and presented their plans to Alex Cooper, Director of the New York City Planning Commission. (The architects had helped develop the Housing Quality Points [HQP] program at Columbia's School of Architecture as a way to encourage the development of small, leftover building sites.) They then applied for a special permit under a 1976 amendment to the ordinance called "Zoning for Housing Quality" that

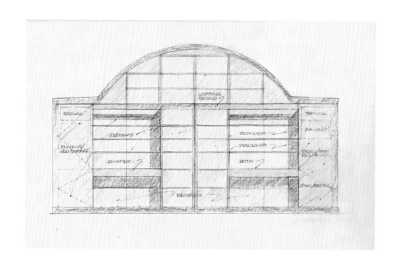

had been adopted as a way to raise aesthetic and practical standards in city housing. Cross ventilation, rooftop play areas for children and additional storage for every unit were among the amenities provided. Under previous zoning rules, the building would have had to have been set back at the eighth floor with thirty feet of open space behind the structure leaving hardly any room on which to build, thus making it impossible to achieve a contextually appropriate height. Smith and Thompson submitted a proposal to construct twelve stories above street level without any setbacks at all. Their supporting argument was that the building, at such a height and flush with the sidewalk property line, would match the rooflines and facades of adjacent historic buildings, thereby achieving the kind of sympathetic synergy that the commission was seeking. The entire south side of the building would be clad in glass with projecting balconies to take advantage of passive solar heating. Retail and professional spaces occupied the lower three floors while living units were designed as flexible dwellings in which rooms could be reconfigured for changing needs and conditions. The standard apartment could be set up with three bedrooms for family use but be easily reconfigured for single-tenant occupancy with open, loft-like plans, or with one and two bedroom options, as desired.

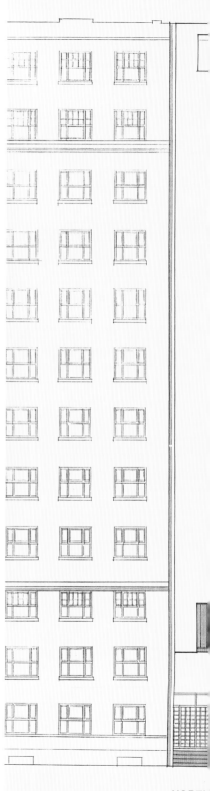

NORTH

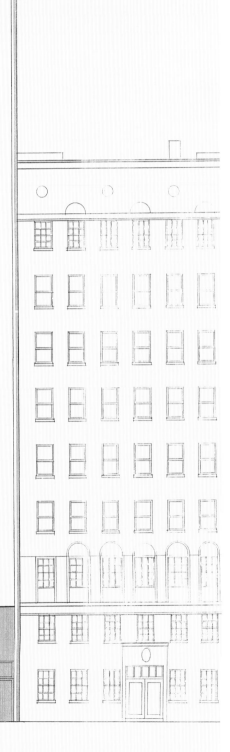

The Planning Commission approved the proposal and praised it for embodying the ideals of the Housing Quality amendment. "If this bulk can be developed on such a constricted site, it would provide high quality housing without detrimental effects on the surrounding neighborhood." [9]

Even though their proposal gained approval from both the commission and the local community planning board, Smith and Thompson were unable to find an investor or developer to bring their plan to completion as the economy was still in recession. They decided to build it themselves in gradual, affordable stages, and after doing the math, calculated that it would be cheaper than renting an equivalent work/live property for their own professional needs.

They broke ground in 1982, excavated a deep well at the back of the lot, and inserted a sub-level office/studio with a large skylight at the rear of the space and a high clerestory window at the north end. In a second phase, carried out a few years later, they added two floor-through apartments corresponding to the HQP's design, for rental income. Now the building rose three stories above the street. Upon completing these additional floors, the architects chose to move their office downtown, but the building at 542 Cathedral Parkway continued to expand as a work in progress and serve as a template in slow-growth design.

In 1987 Smith and Thompson participated in an ideas competition: "Vacant Lots: A Study Project in Infill Housing in New York," that was sponsored by the Architectural League of New York in partnership with the city's Department of Housing Preservation and Development. The idea of the competition (and the subsequent exhibition and book) was to foster creative solutions for low- and moderate-income buildings on ten designated sites in Brooklyn, the Bronx, Queens and Manhattan. The proposal that Smith and Thompson submitted to the competition was conceived for Site #7, a garbage-strewn lot on 133rd Street. The design evolved directly from their Cathedral Parkway scheme with similar workshop spaces at the rear to help inject economic vitality into the neighborhood. Masonry bearing walls with lightweight steel-spanning members were cost effective and could be built by semiskilled workers.[10] Each apartment enclosure was to be assembled by the inhabitant from a palette of materials and window options making the street elevation an exercise in collective individuality.

In 1986, Smith and Thompson were asked to renovate and expand a brownstone on the Upper East Side for Samuel Ornstein, a venture capitalist. The project presented a similar rooftop condition as the Davis Penthouse of 1982. In this case they added two

ALUMNI NEWS

G. PHILLIP SMITH (M.Arch., 1969) and DOUGLAS THOMPSON (M.Arch., 1970) of Smith and Thompson Architects have recently completed a new building to house their offices on Cathedral Parkway in Manhattan. The project also contains three floor-thru apartments that are designed as prototypes for infill housing. The apartments are lofts with two bathrooms, a kitchen and movable partitions that create a range of flexible layouts offering from one to three bedrooms. The project is modeled on designs that the firm submitted as part of the 1989 Architectural League exhibition for the Vacant Lots Infill Housing Competition. The building is engineered to allow construction to a height of 12 stories, and has been granted a special permit under the New York City Housing Quality Points Program.

Smith and Thompson, exterior of 542 Cathedral Parkway, New York, phased construction.

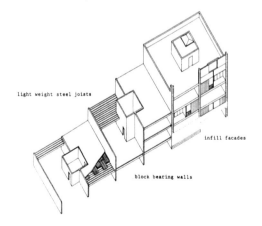

light weight steel joists

infill facades

block bearing walls

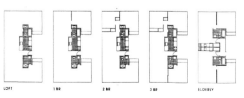

LOFT   1 BR   2 BR   3 BR   ELDERLY

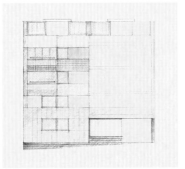

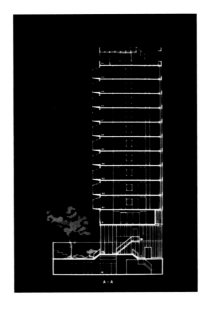

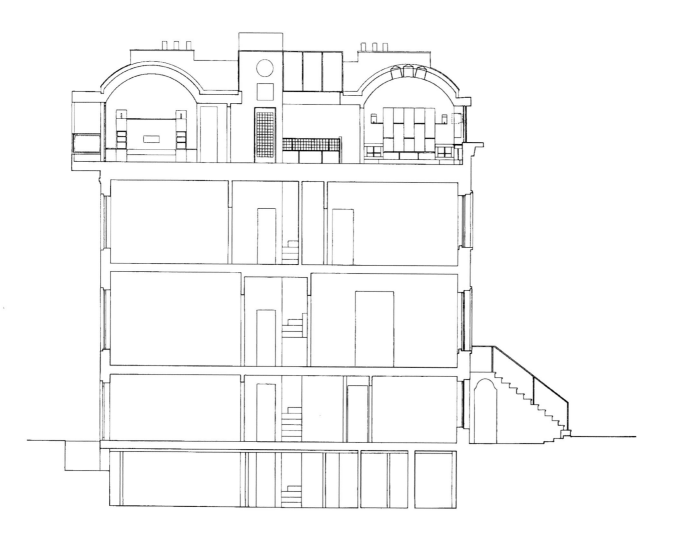

barrel-vaulted pavilions that were similar to the roofs of Doshi's studio in Ahmedabad and Kahn's Kimbell Museum in Fort Worth, Texas. Their brief was to create a master bedroom suite to the south and a bath and exercise area to the north. The idea for the vaulted roof came from a concern for landmarks and zoning issues regarding setbacks and sight lines. Looking up from the street angle, you would only be able to see the low sidewall of the north pavilion while the roof curved back from view. A lower, flat-roofed section connected the vaulted pavilions and provided room for a dressing area and storage beneath an eighteen-foot-long gabled skylight.

PAGE 100:
Vacant Lots Competition proposal, W 133rd Street, New York City, 1987

PAGE 101:
Stages of progress, 542 Cathedral Parkway, New York City, 1976-1985

BOTH PAGES:
Ornstein Townhouse, E 69th Street, New York City, 1986

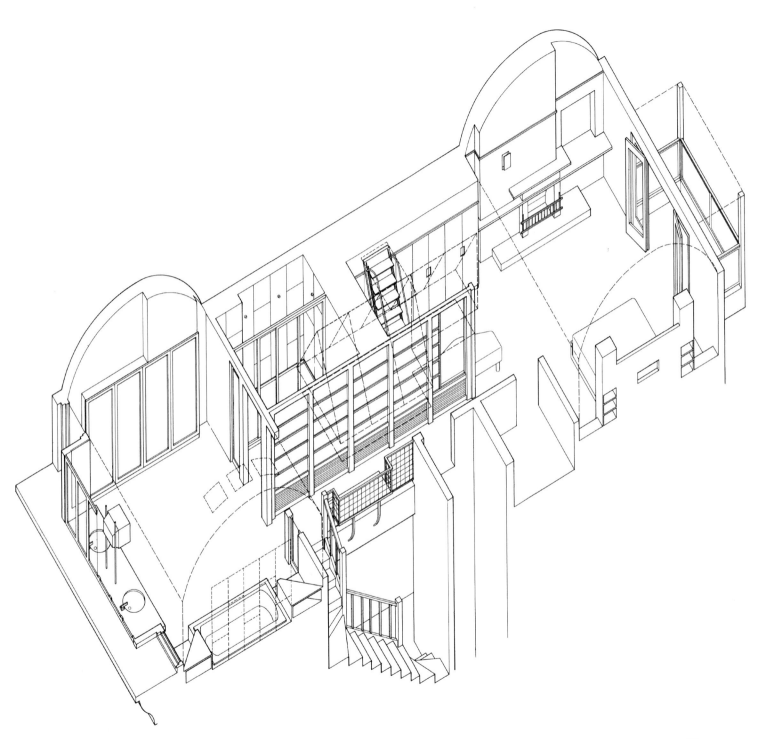

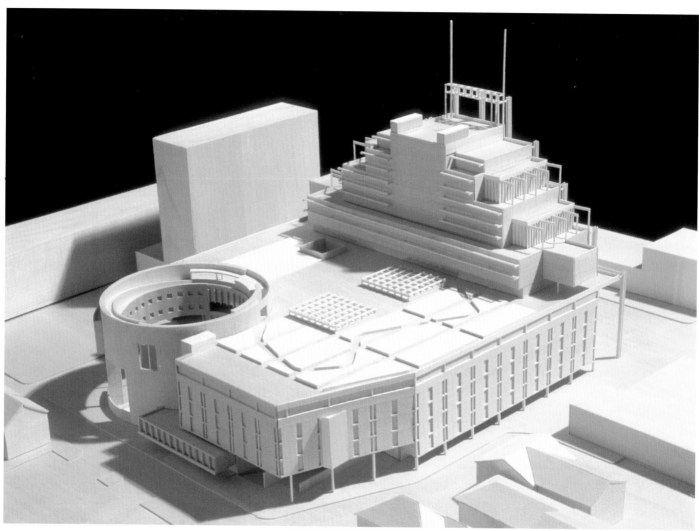

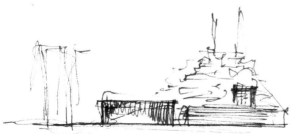

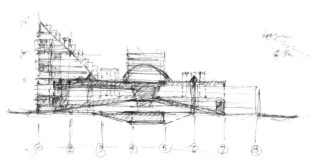

With stepped-back tower and pronounced radio masts, the Mobile County Courthouse (1990, Alabama) echoes the bridge of a supertanker moored out on Mobile Bay. It also expresses a strident complexity of program that recalls the Constructivism of Konstantin Melnikov's Soviet Pavilion and Le Corbusier's Palace of Soviets. The message here is not social revolution, however, but civic stability. (In fact, the firm's inspiration for this tapering, clustered edifice was the pink sandstone Hawa Mahal, or "Palace of the Winds," in Jaipur, India, that was designed in the 18th century as sleeping porches for the Maharaja's concubines.) The main entrance, at the southwest corner, provides a welcoming, open-air rotunda that leads into the various law courts, library, county offices and mayor's offices, all arranged around two large atriums. This five-story section has a roof landscaped with thick hedges, a running track and gardens. The north side of the courthouse has a symmetrical colonnade that addresses the colonial streetscape of Government Boulevard with its Greek Revival facades and neoclassical porticos. A grid-work of steel framing, something like an oversized trellis, effectively extends the lines of the building out into the street, while multi-tiered balconies provide viewing platforms for the public and judges during the annual Mardi Gras parade that passes down the boulevard.

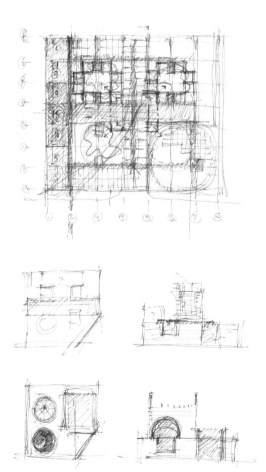

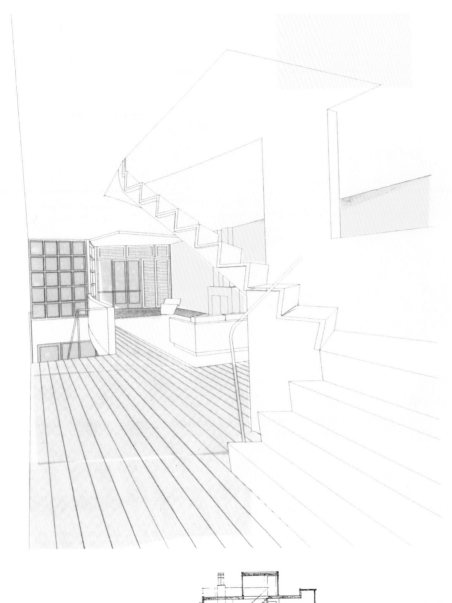

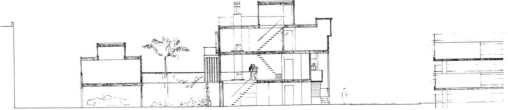

BOTH PAGES :
Interior sketch, section,
plans and models of
Warren Square Townhouses,
Savannah, Georgia, 1994-96

PAGES 108-109:
Model and Elevation study,
Warren Square Townhouses

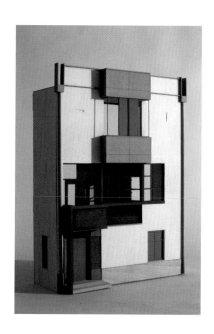

For the Warren Square Townhouses in Savannah, Georgia (1996), the architects were obliged to work within Savannah's rich historic district in a way that echoed the roof heights and scale of neighboring buildings while remaining modern in character. Smith and Thompson's approach to the site evolved directly from their work on Cathedral Parkway and the urban infill ideas competition of 1987. Each of the five townhouses included a three-story residence facing out onto East Congress Street. A smaller, two-story guesthouse and a two-car garage would be accessible from the traditional mid-block alley in the citywide plan. A 23-foot-square courtyard and garden separated the two structures. Facades were articulated with French doors, gridded windows, overhangs and slatted shutters. A small balcony and oversized bay window looked out over the garden from the master bedroom suite on the second floor. Roofs were flat with terraces and modest penthouses for rooftop relaxation, an innovation for Savannah. Interiors were open and free flowing, more like lofts than conventional townhouses. The light-filled living areas had soaring, ten-foot-high ceilings.

While their townhouse design would have made for an appropriately contextual contemporary building, it became a local controversy and caused an extended review process, much as the East Hampton Airport project had done. In this case, a final approval was granted by the Historic District Commission (HDC) after several revised submissions and two years of further presentations. An ensuing economic downturn, however, caused the client to shelve the project indefinitely.

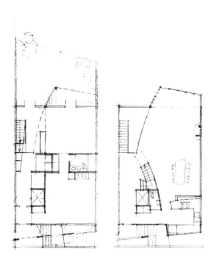

109

Still in search of the ideal site for an experimental live/work project, Smith and Thompson were riding their bikes around Manhattan, looking for affordable lots. One Sunday morning they turned off the West Side Highway at 23rd Street, pedaling east, and noticed a vacant lot on the corner of 10th Avenue. "We came screeching to a halt when we saw the 'For Sale' sign," Smith said. "It was love at first sight." The property had formerly been the site of two brownstones demolished for tax reasons and then turned into a parking lot. It measured 54 by 40 feet and seemed like the perfect size for their needs so they decided that this would be where they'd build their dream building.[11]

They liked the rough-edged nature of the light-manufacturing neighborhood that included a gas station on one corner, elevated train tracks to the west (later to become the High Line Park,) as well as local landmarks like the Empire Diner and the London Terrace apartment complex located directly across 10th Avenue.

The architects phoned the real estate broker early the next morning and learned that the property had just gone to contract, but they asked the agent to keep them informed of any future activity. "We let her know that we were very excited about building on this property," Thompson said. After three years of waiting, their patience paid off. The lot came back on the market for five times the original price. This time, with a short-term construction loan, and armed with a drawer full of credit cards (which they quickly maxed out), the architects were able to buy it and begin making plans.

"Remember," Smith said, "none of this had anything to do with real estate speculation. We weren't interested in maximizing the site for profit. We wanted to make a beautiful place."

They sketched ideas on napkins and tablecloths, designing an approximately 5,400-square-foot building that would provide several different functions: a domestic living space, a design studio for the architects, and rental spaces to help defer costs. They chose to under build so that they could retain control of the process and avoid having to bring in financial partners. All the elements would be joined together in a cube-like accretion of interior spaces, voids, courtyards and terraces, a self-contained oasis set within a frenetic urban environment.

"At one point we thought about just living like gypsies on the site," Thompson said, "parking a trailer and building a swimming pool. Then we could drive away whenever we felt restless." Gradually, a more permanent and practical concept evolved, one that acknowledged, even honored, the pace and geometric pressures of the city grid.

OPPOSITE:
Gallery Building, Construction
of steel framework

ABOVE:
Inspiration: Engraving of
a vernacular 18th century
residence, Cairo

"Most people think of Manhattan as a closed, finite kind of space with the grid as the dominant force," said Smith. "We wanted to acknowledge that grid while inserting a fluid sequence of spaces within an enclosed area."

They knew from the start that there had to be a courtyard to serve as a transition from public to private domains, and accommodate a mature sycamore tree that grew next to the building lot. (They'd seen this done for similarly venerable trees in traditional Asian courtyard buildings.) They also wanted to establish a landmark presence on the corner of 23rd and 10th, with two or more stories, respecting the lines of the street and giving the structure an inner transparency.

One of the most important touchstones for the architects during the early period of conception was the Noguchi Museum that opened in 1985, around the same time that Smith and Thompson were beginning to think about their new studio. The museum was housed in an old factory in Long Island City with a sculpture garden and a series of galleries for showcasing Noguchi's sculptures. "It was one of our favorite places in the city," said Thompson. "Once inside the central courtyard, exterior and interior spaces flowed into one another in such a seamless, elegant way."

Another influence was the antique etching they owned of a classically vernacular residence in Cairo, Egypt, an L-shaped building that organized itself around a courtyard for both public and private functions, with balconies and terraces. "It was extremely rich in plan and elevation, with so many different levels of interest," said Thompson.

From the beginning, the architects sought an economy of means and flexibility in the construction process. After completing drawings, they acted as their own general contractors and orchestrated all phases of construction so as to remain in touch with the process and save on costs. After foundation work was finished, a framework of steel I-beams was bolted and welded into place like a jungle gym. The steel plates took only a single day to install because they'd all been precut and stacked on the delivery truck in the order of assembly. Additional money was saved by using cold-rolled steel as it came directly off the mill, in precut, ten-by-twenty-foot sheets. The size of the plates established a ten-foot-square modular that the architects applied throughout the project. (It also happened to fit the dimensions of the building lot.)

Smith and Thompson searched through stacks of steel with an eye for the most interesting surfaces. "Every steel mill has a unique finish," Thompson said. "Most come out fairly black." A set of plates from a mill in Pennsylvania had a consistent powdery red finish, a kind of cordovan color that they liked. They rented a crane and all went

LOWER LEFT:
Gallery Building at dusk, 2009

LOWER RIGHT:
Template for tree cut-out

OPPOSITE, ABOVE:
Original Study, Gallery Building

OPPOSTIE, BELOW:
Travel sketches, Phillip Smith

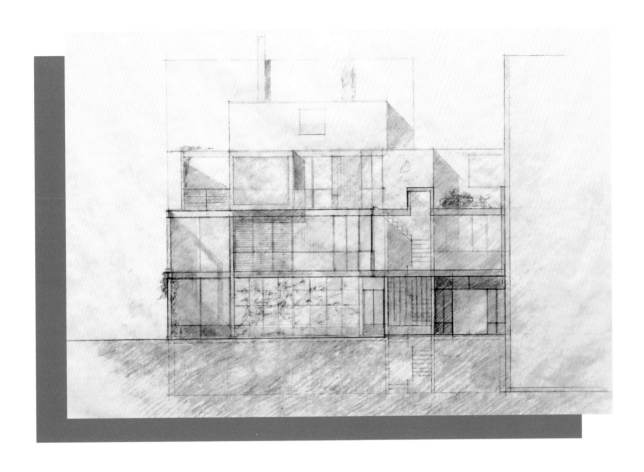

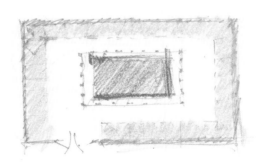

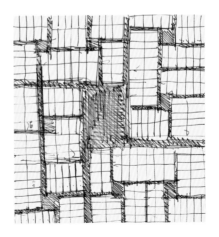

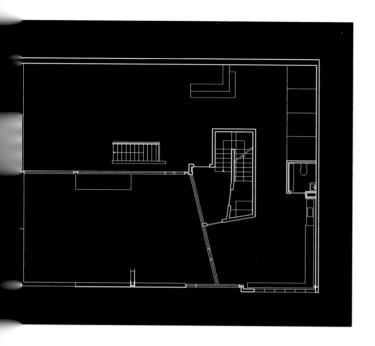

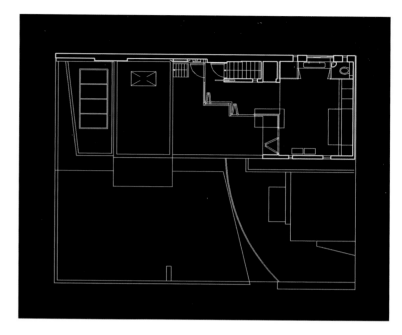

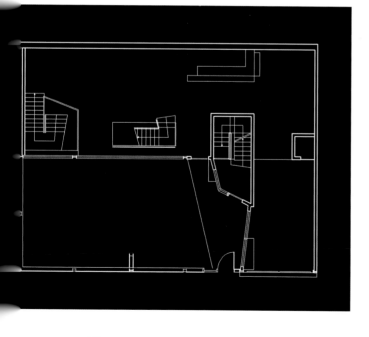

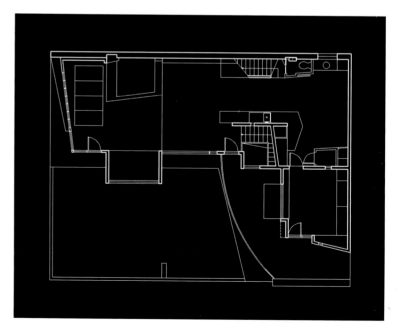

116

OPPOSITE, LEFT:
Plans of lower gallery floors

OPPOSITE, RIGHT:
Plans of upper floors,
Smith and Thompson Studio

BELOW:
Concealed storage and
fold-up workstations in Smith
and Thompson Studio

PAGE 118, LEFT:
Sculpture garden from
second floor

PAGE 119, RIGHT:
Sculpture garden from the
street

well until the last steel plate was uncovered, the one with an opening for the sycamore branch. Even though the fabricator had been given accurate measurements of the aperture, there was only a five-inch notch instead of a much larger opening as designed by Smith and Thompson who quickly hand sketched the proper outline onto the steel and watched as one of the installers cut the opening into the plate with a hand torch.

After exterior walls were in place, the steel was coated with a paraffin-based sealer to prevent rusting and protect against graffiti. Heavy-duty timber framing was used for the rest of the structural infill, allowing for ease of reframing alternate staircase connections in the future. In some places, gray and white stucco panels were incorporated to create a contrast with the dark steel. Cubic elements were stacked like blocks so that different spaces could be combined and recombined over time and be easily adapted to changing functions.

The courtyard and two gallery spaces on the lower floors were finished first, in 1997. Several restaurants expressed interest in renting and while this would have provided higher revenues, Smith and Thompson wanted sympathetic neighbors in their village compound. The J. Cacciola Galleries moved from Soho into the ground-floor space. Jim Kempner Fine Arts also left SoHo and moved into the second floor. "The building is helping us all to be together," Smith said. "It's really like a small community."

PAGES 120–121:
Private quarters on
upper floor of Smith and
Thompson studio

OPPOSITE:
Bernar Venet sculpture in
garden

ABOVE:
Gallery on first floor, detail of
steel staircase

As you approach from the west, it appears to be hovering like a lantern in the late October twilight and seems rice-paper thin at first, almost too insubstantial for such a noisy, intense setting, more like a temporary pavilion erected for a fair or circus. Where are the defensive barriers, the thick walls and narrow entry points that normally signal the line between public and private space? They are almost nonexistent.

Getting closer, you begin to see that the effect is a deliberately composed illusion. The perimeter walls are not paper after all, but armor-plated steel and everything changes when you step through the portal and enter the courtyard. Even though the outer membrane is only a quarter-inch thick, street noises are muffled substantially, and it's surprisingly peaceful, almost meditative. The city is still out there, rude and clamorous, but it seems distant and remote. Everything fits into the cubic framework of solid and void, except the parabolic opening that accommodates the tree branch. The floor of the courtyard is covered with gravel. Pavers, made from recycled plastic decking, have been placed like stepping stones in a Japanese garden.

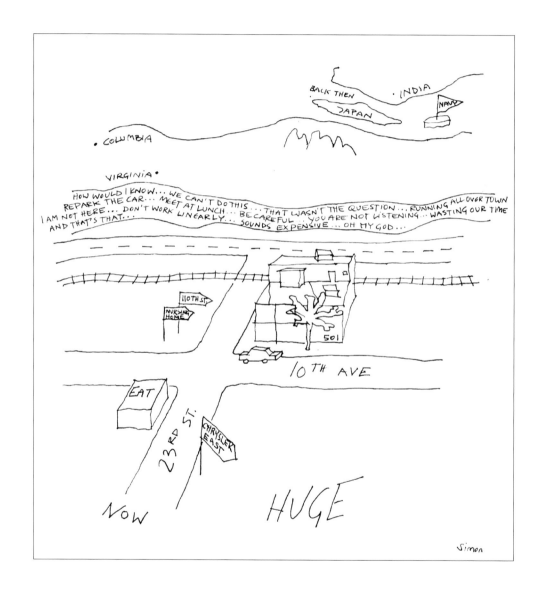

For such a relatively small structure, there are several overlapping narratives going on, but each space leads to the next with a clarity of intent. One is aware of the sky and the dramas being played out on the sidewalk. Lines of sight were intentionally arranged to create a play between privacy and exposure, light and shadow, transparency and opacity. Multiple views and openings divide and transform the action on the outside of the building into a series of small theatrical events that even incorporate advertisements on the side of a passing bus, pedestrians, the flash of a yellow cab, all glimpsed fleetingly through the slit-like openings.

Conventional borders were further dissolved by the way the architects arranged their studio on the third floor. A system of "Murphy desks" fold up into the wall so that the space can be open for art exhibits, photo shoots, and entertaining on the weekends. Then there is a small research library loft which hovers above the design studio and a folded steel plate staircase that ascends to a more recently completed fourth floor for Smith and Thompson's private use. This level includes one of two roof terraces that look out over the busy intersection of 23rd Street and 10th Avenue.

The building continues to grow as a work in progress with new spaces set back like rooms of a pueblo village rising in tiers toward the naked wall of an adjacent building.

"This process is completely open ended," Smith says. "The building continues to unfold."

OPPOSITE:
Steinberg-inspired drawing of Smith and Thompson studio by Simon Fellmeth

ABOVE:
Gallery Building with neon sculpture by Antonakos

RIGHT:
Sketch studies for 5th floor addition

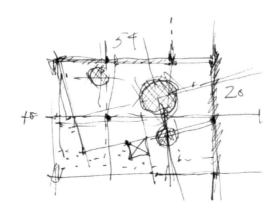

125

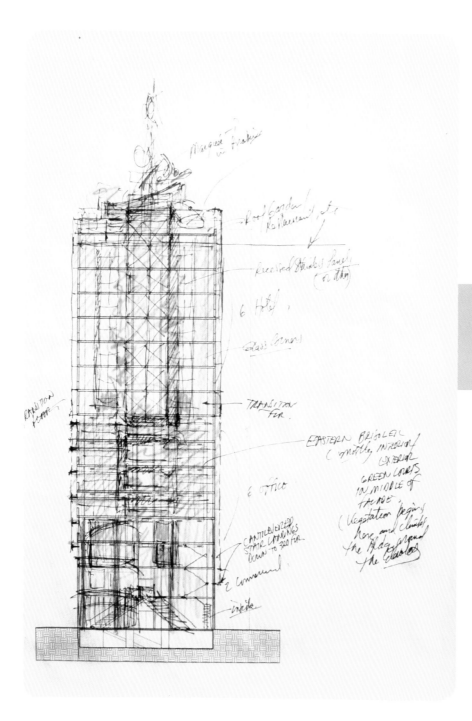

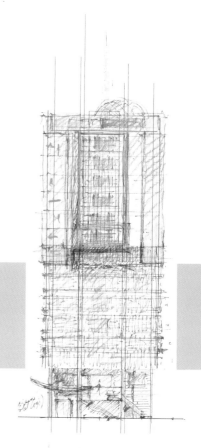

In 2003, Smith and Thompson were commissioned to design the Agrabad, a "destination" hotel in Chittagong, Bangladesh. The high-rise project combines hotel accommodations with a government trade center and mixed-use commercial space on the lower levels to help finance the project. The main lobby is located on the seventh floor with independent glass-enclosed elevators placed on the arrival facade of Agrabad Road, the main axial street that runs through the heart of Chittagong. Rooms have double-glazed exterior closures with balconies layered between the two. The glass facade acts as a sun and purdah screen. Rooftop facilities include a restaurant, lounge, and strolling gardens for evening relaxation. The east elevation is a living wall of plants that shades the elevator lobbies and acts as a significant landmark in the urban landscape. When complete, the sixteen-floor building will be the tallest in Chittagong.

EPIPHANY

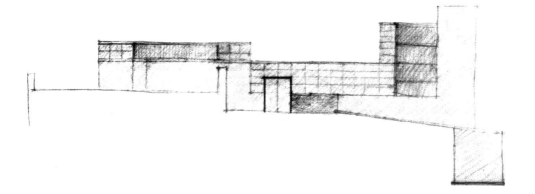

PAGES 128-129:
Model of the Jacques
Marchais Museum of Tibetan
Art, Staten Island,
New York City, 1995

ABOVE:
The original museum built by
Jacques Marchais in 1947

BELOW:
Section study for the
Museum of Tibetan Art

OPPOSITE, ABOVE:
Elevation from the downhill
side

OPPOSITE, BELOW:
Early travel sketch,
Phillip Smith

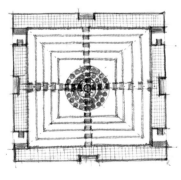

"We knew we would find the solution to the problem in the natural landscape," said Smith and Thompson regarding their work on the Jacques Marchais Museum of Tibetan Art, which was founded in 1945 to promote the study of Tibetan culture. Jacques Marchais (aka Mrs. Jacqueline Klauber) built two stone buildings on Staten Island to house her extensive collection of artifacts. (She died in 1947, soon after completion of the first phase of building.) The site presents a steep hillside that drops nine stories from Lighthouse Avenue to Nugent Street below. Original buildings were modeled after traditional Tibetan chanting halls with Tibetan-style windows, terraced sculpture garden, fishpond, and panoramic views of the Lower Bay.

Smith and Thompson began work on a master plan for the restoration and expansion of the museum in 1995, with the idea of preserving the chanting hall at the heart of the complex and turning the existing rooftop into an entry terrace that would effectively connect the street and garden levels. More space was needed for a library, exhibitions,

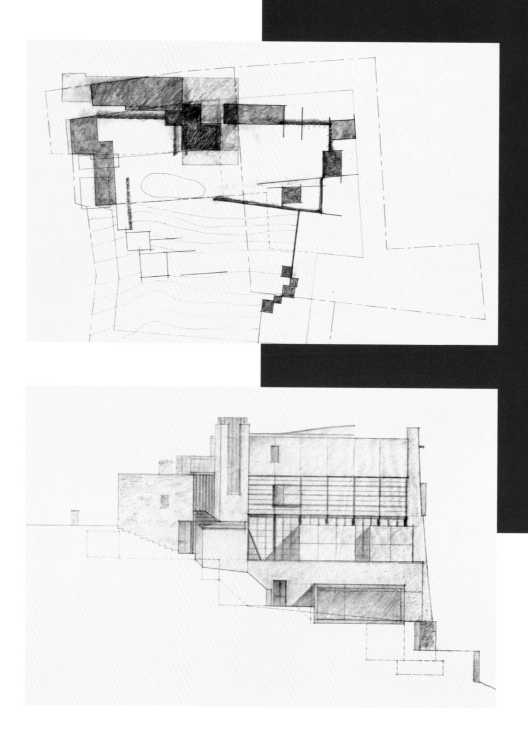

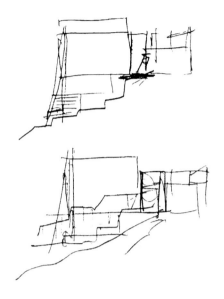

administration and curatorial facilities as well as an apartment for visiting monks and the Dalai Lama. Rather than imposing a single, monolithic structure on the site, they chose to break up the scale and create a series of smaller, incremental components that could be linked by a meandering kind of circulation, more like a pathway through a garden than a conventional, foursquare building. "In this way, the museum experience would be active and ambulatory and would take full advantage of the drama of the site," said Thompson.

The architects studied the fortified monasteries of Tibet--Kampa Dzong in southern Tibet, Trashilungpo Monastery in Shigaste, Sakya Monastery and the Potola Palace in Lhasa--a building typology that was shaped over hundreds of years by small changes, gradually expanding and reaching out into the natural landscape with "battered" walls and irregular additions generated over time to accommodate the needs of the monks and in response to the severe terrain and weather of Tibet. The architects took note of how the bases of these monasteries were always heavy and grounded while the architectural massing grew more ephemeral and multipartite as it mounted higher with smaller pavilions, wooden balconies, porches and towers.

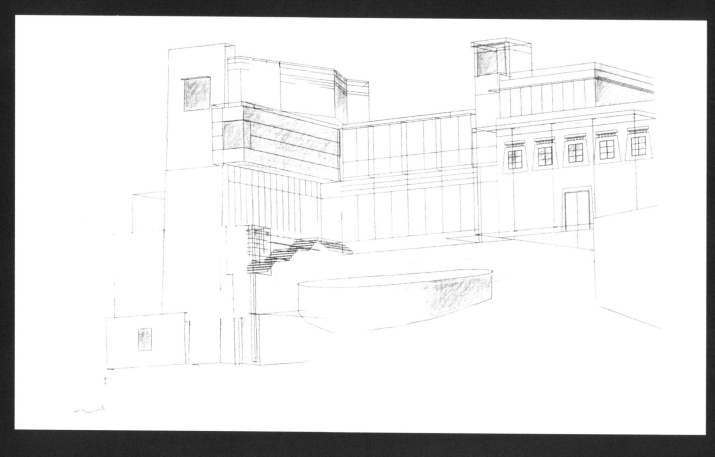

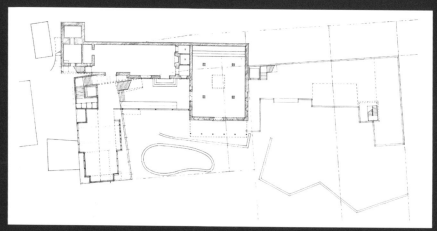

While keeping within the same vernacular scale of parts, Smith and Thompson introduced a much less literal (and less decorative) interpretation of Tibetan building vocabulary than the pre-existing buildings on Staten Island. The old museum building was incorporated into the new design, surrounded, embraced and expanded with thoroughly modern, pared-down but suggestive shapes, textures and surface treatments.

The acute steepness of the site suggested upward thrusting verticals anchored by grounded horizontality: towers, terraces, and galleries rising up in stacked layers. New additions were planned in gradual phases in accordance with the institution's fund-raising schedule. "Each phase could be a stopping point or a resolved increment, much in the way that Tibetan monasteries were built by accretion," wrote Smith and Thompson in their proposal. They worked with landscape architects Margaret Ruddick and Judith Heintz to create an alternate, zigzagging "pilgrimage route" up the hill to the museum from Nugent Street.

"Just as a pilgrimage reveals events along the way, so too would the visitor encounter different chapels and terraces that would be a preview of the experience to come," said Smith.

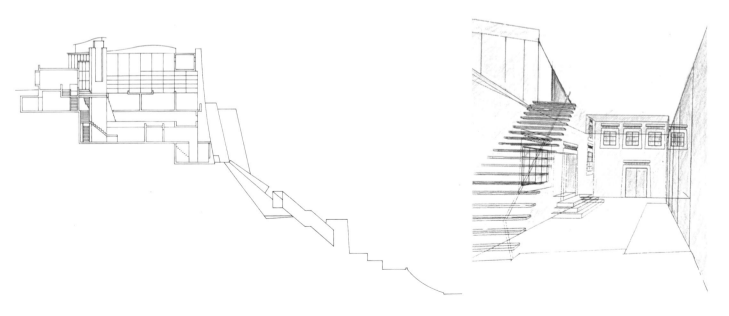

As with their 23rd Street studio, there's a rhythmic fracturing of the museum's bulk into smaller volumes--loggias, porches, belvederes--rising above the roofline, poking out, and sloping back into the hillside, creating a highly articulated facade from the south and east that echoes the interwoven texture of classic Tibetan architecture and the worlds-within-worlds of traditional Thangka painting. A multiplicity of parts are revealed while others are hidden or partially concealed by gridded wooden screens, translucent panels, veil-like walls and overhanging balconies to create a rippling surface effect of greater depth and chiaroscuro. Parts are broken down and rearranged with discrete identities within a greater whole: ramps and stairs, balustrades and buttresses, terraces, walkways and loggias negotiate the rise with steps and terraces for reflective moments while always considering the attendant views.

Another project with a similarly spiritual program was the New York Buddhist Church. The church purchased the former Hearst Mansion at 105th Street and Riverside Drive, adjacent to their existing building, and commissioned Smith and Thompson in 1990 to prepare a master plan that would integrate the historic property with the adjoining sanctuary building that had been built in 1953. They were also asked to reconfigure and

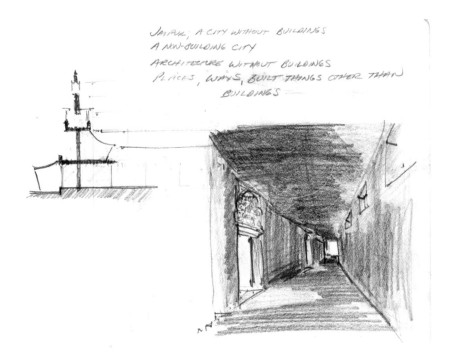

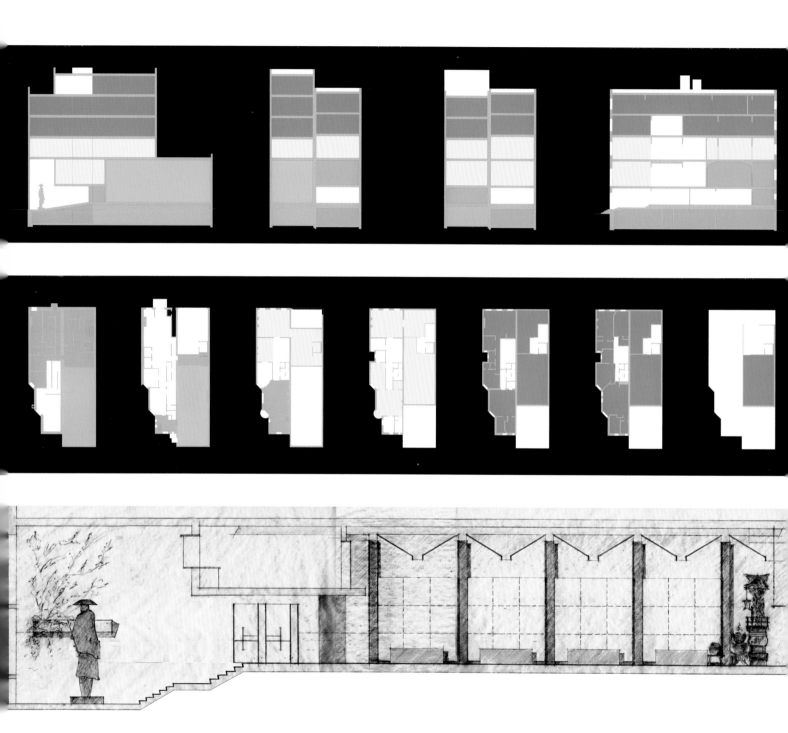

142

renovate the Hearst building to provide spaces for classes, a library, tea ceremony, dance performances, and dormitory-like bedrooms for visiting monks as well as a minister's apartment. The renovation of the Hearst Mansion was completed in 1993. Subsequently, they designed a four-story expansion above the sanctuary. "We wanted to stretch the facade as high as possible to continue the street presence of the historic Beaux Arts mansion," said Thompson. They would use a screen wall made from mesh and operable louvers to take advantage of solar heating. Again, as with the Tibetan Museum, the idea was to take traditional vernacular--in this case the Zen Buddhist temples of Kyoto, Japan--and create a modern remix of those traditions.

Outside the building stands a statue of Shinran Shonin, the founder of the Jodo Shinshu school of Buddhism. (This particular statue survived the atomic bombing of Hiroshima.) In 2007, the architects began work on a new "Hondo" sanctuary space to replace the existing one while adding new mechanical and structural systems for a future four-story addition to house offices, a library and roof garden with a green roof.

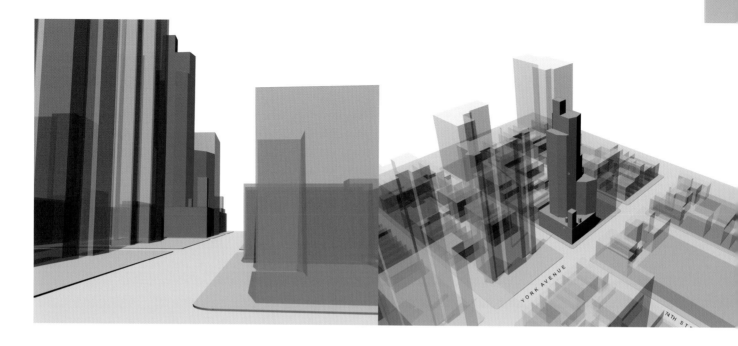

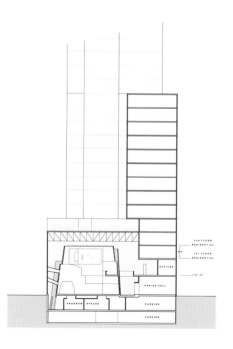

In 2006, Smith and Thompson were asked to prepare a space planning study for the Episcopal Church of the Epiphany. Church elders wanted to develop a property they owned at 1393 York Avenue by building a new church on the ground level and a residential high-rise above to help endow the church's homeless and medical outreach program as well as its day school. The plan was to allow flexible space and advanced technical equipment for an international meeting facility to be known as the Epiphany Forum. The architects wanted to create a sacred space that felt highly visible and accessible so that people on the street would feel welcome. Smith and Thompson worked closely with a zoning consultant to determine the size and shape of the structure, a process that was complicated by the fact that the property in question straddled two different zoning lots. Taking a lesson from Le Corbusier's pyramidal church at Saint-Pierre de Firminy, there would be a "soft," organically shaped space with a side chapel, sacristy and vestry encased within a transparent glass envelope and placed in the most conspicuous position on the corner of 74th Street and York Avenue. A large ceremonial gate could be opened on special occasions to reveal the curved exterior shell of the sanctuary. The York Avenue arrival elevation would peel away toward the encased sanctuary and thereby create a congregational flow from the street around and into the sanctuary and adjacent public spaces. The day school would look out onto a landscaped garden from the second level.

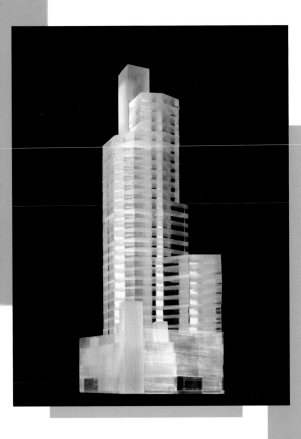

OPPOSITE, ABOVE:
Perspective and massing
study of Church of the
Epiphany project,
New York City, 2006

OPPOSITE, BELOW:
Section of church facilities in
the required base building

ABOVE, RIGHT:
Plexiglas model and
rendering of Church of the
Epiphany project

145

OPPOSITE:
Conceptual sketch of Church
of the Epiphany

RIGHT:
Early model of Church of the
Epiphany

BELOW:
Blenko blown glass sanctuary
rondelles

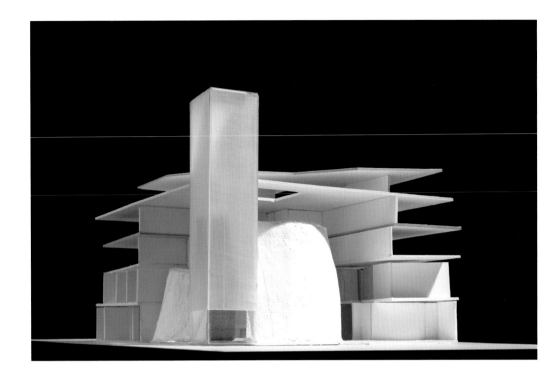

In their competition entry for the expansion of the Queens Museum of Art (2002), Smith and Thompson incorporated vestigial gestures and themes already present in the former World's Fair grounds at Flushing Meadows Corona Park. They created a digitally enhanced glass facade for the front entrance and a grass-ramped amphitheater that faces the original 1964 Unisphere Theme Center. Their circulation plan was based on the walkway system that currently encircles the panorama model of New York City that was originally presented in the New York City Pavilion as part of the 1964/65 World's Fair. Administration and curatorial spaces were located on a lower level and topped by skylights that borrow light from a large central atrium while permanent exhibitions and other gallery spaces are located around the perimeter of a large public forum. A gallery for temporary exhibits is suspended above with connecting bridges to the surrounding galleries. A rooftop sculpture gallery and garden offers dramatic views of the surrounding park and out past the Grand Central Parkway to Flushing Bay. The rooftop garden can be reached by an oversized exterior elevator that was patterned after the hangar-bay elevators found on aircraft carriers. The digital displays on the glass facade entry wall carry an ever-changing stream of information about current exhibits and events.

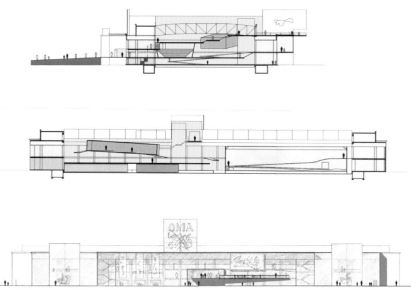

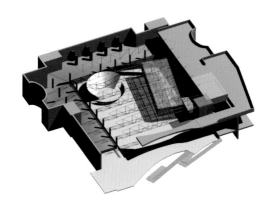

The High Line, adjacent to Smith and Thompson's studio, offered one of the most fruitful urban reclamations of the past decade. When a competition was announced to renovate and repurpose the former elevated railway, Smith and Thompson responded with an extended kind of pedestrian boardwalk--as in a seaside promenade--a new kind of horizontal framework to reconfigure and revitalize this formerly industrial area of lower Manhattan with landscaping for multiple kinds of urban interaction. It would unify the 1.5-mile length of elevated railway to include lawns, water gardens as well as large steel trellises with seasonal plantings, translucent screens with projected imagery and monumental sculptures interspersed along its track. An amphitheater and restaurants are located at the two points where the park crosses 10th Avenue. Entry points are placed every three blocks and are announced by glass-enclosed elevators and stairwells that support solar collector canopies that will provide energy for the functions of the High Line. Gatehouses at each end of the promenade provide highly visible points of access--the South Gate with galleries and a rooftop garden, the North Gate at 30th Street with a domed winter garden. Street crossings are lightened by replacing sections of the concrete roadbed with glass set into the surface as well as new lighting under the crossings. Businesses adjacent to the High Line are encouraged to link up and interact with the linear spectacle of the new park.

OPPOSITE:
The Queens Museum Competition, New York City, 2002

THIS PAGE:
The Highline Competition, New York City, 2003

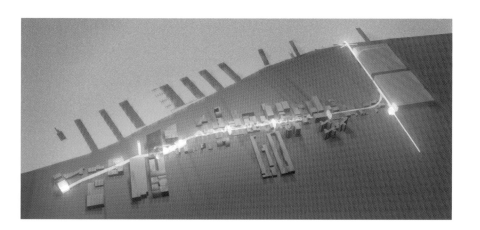

Renderings, plans and
elevation for the Miami
Seaplane Base Competition,
Miami, Florida, 2010

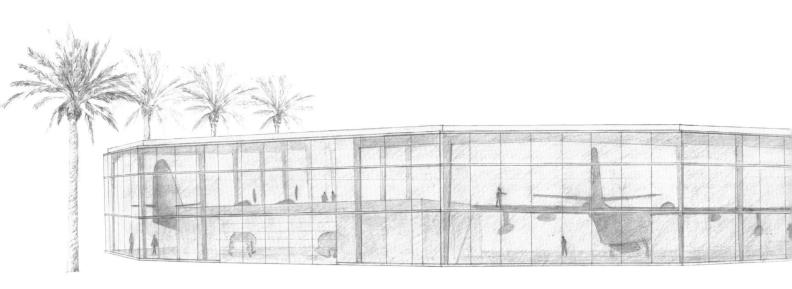

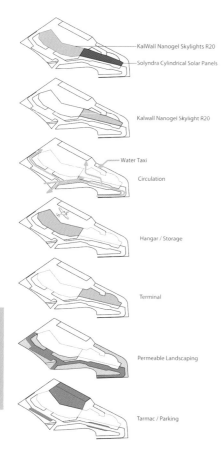

KalWall Nanogel Skylights R20

Solyndra Cylindrical Solar Panels

Kalwall Nanogel Skylight R20

Water Taxi

Circulation

Hangar / Storage

Terminal

Permeable Landscaping

Tarmac / Parking

All programmatic elements for the Miami Seaplane Base competition of 2010 were gathered together under a single, 450-foot overarching roof made up of sweeping skylights and tubular solar collectors. The long, eccentrically shaped pavilion was designed for a waterfront site on Watson Island and lies astride MacArthur Causeway in the middle of Biscayne Bay. The terminal is constructed of sheer glass walls and translucent Kalwall ceilings that reflect the lightness and luminosity of flight while creating a gallery-like setting for the aircraft. The plan itself echoes the aerodynamic lines of a modern airframe and bends back from the bay with twin hangars, entry atrium, waiting room and administrative offices. The open and flexible plan allows panoramic views of approaching planes and downtown Miami's skyline. The building follows the shoreline of the Government Cut where passengers arrive by water taxi. Walkways are landscaped with tropical plantings and vistas are maintained to the east and west. Vehicular traffic arrives in a landscaped courtyard on the north side. The ideas competition has fostered the discussion of how to accommodate the seaplanes into the urban fabric of downtown Miami.

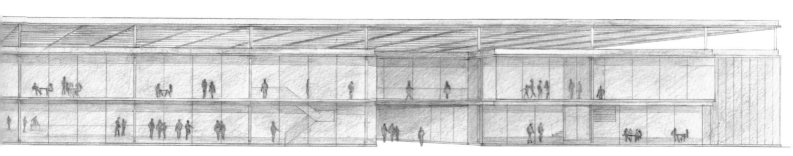

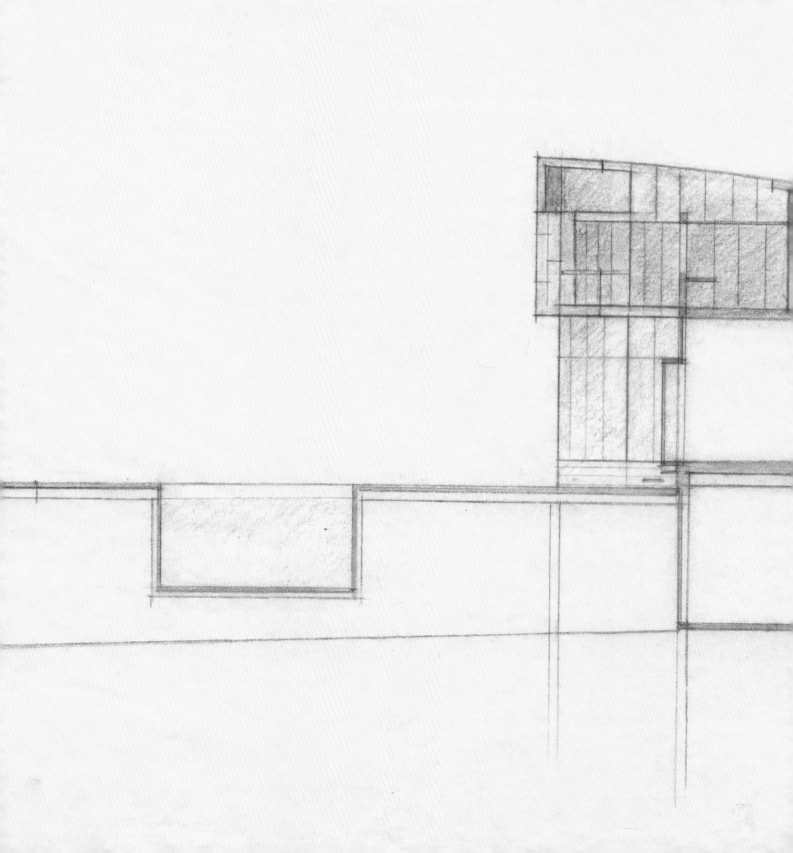

DECOMPRESSION

PAGE 152-153:
Section of Fisher Residence

PAGES 154-155:
Fisher Residence,
Dune Road, Westhampton,
New York, 2007

ABOVE, LEFT:
Three story stairwell

ABOVE, RIGHT:
Window overlooking the
ocean

OPPOSITE, ABOVE:
Detail of translucent screen

OPPOSITE, BELOW:
Plan of 2nd floor and section

The wave-like roofline of the Fisher House (2007) advances and then recedes like the surf, as it negotiates the narrow strip of sand between the Atlantic Ocean on one side and Moriches Bay on the other. The interlocking forms of this 3,300-square-foot weekend house evoke the sand dunes and hovering, sea-flecked skies of eastern Long Island. They also express more of a single, sweeping gesture compared to the additive accretions that characterize many of Smith and Thompson's other residential projects.

The house steps away from the road in three different bays, each with a protruding balcony with clerestory windows above. For most of the summer, this narrow sandbar on Westhampton Beach is peaceful and benign but it can also be inundated by hurricane floods and battered by devastating winds, so there is a degree of risk and an inherent

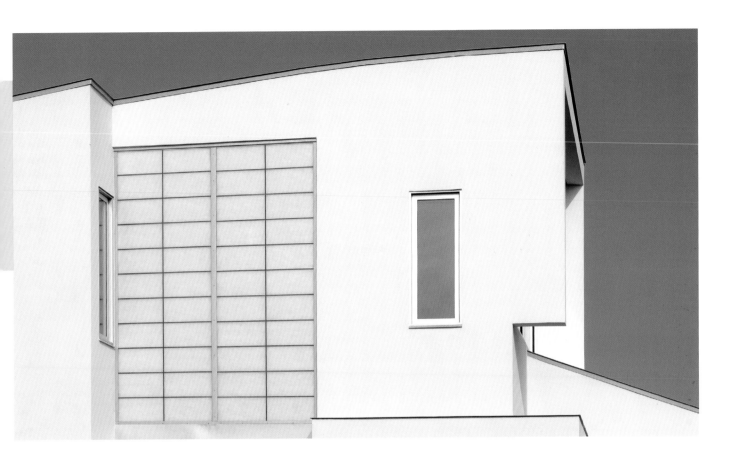

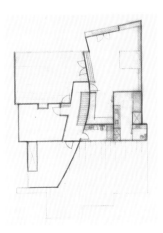

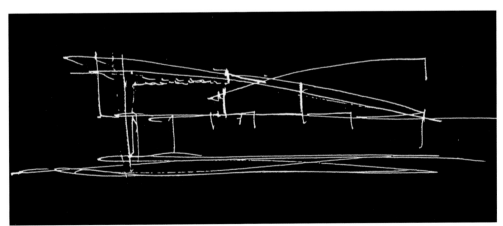

PAGE 158:
Living area

PAGE 159:
Solar tracking window
louvers

LEFT:
Central hall

OPPOSITE:
Kitchen and dining area

challenge being made to the elements. The palette is neutral: pewter seamed-roof and white walls that defer to the natural shades of sea, sky and salt-water marsh, but also act as a foil for reflecting light and the shadows of passing clouds. Fenestration at adjacent property lines was reduced to fairly minimal openings and translucent infill materials to obscure views of neighboring houses. There are vertical and horizontal slits to the east and an almost fully opaque wall with a three-story translucent screen of Kalwall to the west.

A long ramp leads to the main entrance and interior spaces reflect a similar kind of "pulling through" of energy and light from the ocean to the bayside with an entry sequence that curves to the left, echoing the movement of the roof, then leads into a large and open living area that, in turn, spills out to a deck and swimming pool through floor-to-ceiling windows. Guest rooms are located in a 'house within a house' on the main floor, each with their own exterior balcony. Cabinetwork is made from ash with a pale, driftwood stain in contrast to the charcoal-stained bamboo floors. The interior staircase picks up the same curving, wave-like motion as the entry hall and leads to the master bedroom and an outdoor living deck on the second floor with a fireplace sheltered by glass windscreens. Passive solar heating is provided by large expanses of thermally protected low-e glazing placed for optimum efficiency in the winter and necessary protection in the summer. Tall, motorized aluminum blades screen large windows to the west.

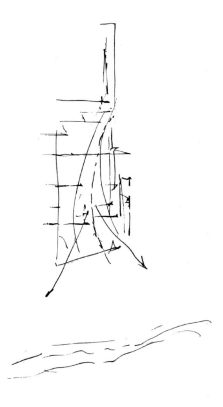

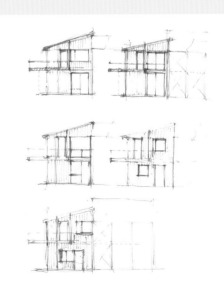

The Siegel House (1994) was built on the site of an old farmstead in a heavily wooded plateau outside of Red Hook, New York, with rock escarpments and a cliff. It was designed for a sculptor and psychiatrist who wanted to build the house themselves and started by clearing an opening among the evergreens while retaining as many existing trees as possible. The house was sited to overlook a pond and a series of earth sculptures designed by the homeowner. Similar in some ways to Smith and Thompson's own house in East Hampton, the plan is elongated with a number of separate sections and towers, not unlike the extended farmhouses of New England vernacular. It extends a series of fractured sections into a kind of intermediary screen between cliffside and pond. Two twenty-by-twenty-foot cubic volumes anchor the horizontal composition. The entrance hall is lengthened and widened to gallery proportions for the display of the owner's laminated-paper sculptures. The gallery creates the axis from which the rest of the house unfolds. A playful, tree house feeling was enhanced by a stair tower that reaches upwards and outwards to a grove of hemlocks. The exterior is clad with paper-coated MDO board, commonly used for signboards. The relative economy and simplicity of this material was juxtaposed with cedar siding to enrich and punctuate certain exterior areas such as an east-facing wall that adjoins an outdoor terrace area. A large screened-in porch next to the kitchen also extends the house and engages the site. Interior and exterior trim and window mullions were made from cedar that was strengthened on the longer spans of glazing by sandwiching them with structural steel framing. Floors are radiant-heated concrete slabs set almost flush with grade to minimize the differential between inside and outside. The floor slab absorbs solar radiation in the winter months while the garage and studio protect the northern exposure in the manner of early regional saltbox houses.

OPPOSITE, ABOVE:
**Siegel Residence,
Red Hook, New York, 1994**

OPPOSITE, BELOW:
Model and sketches

RIGHT:
Elevation rendering

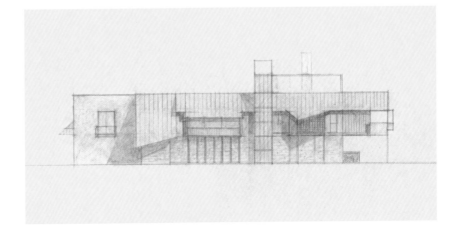

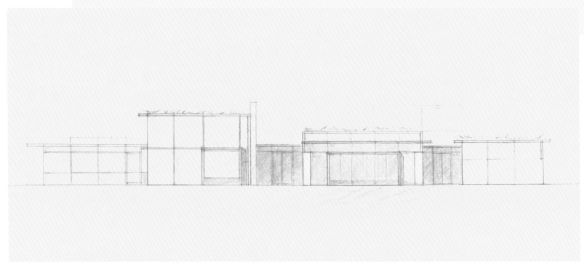

The Resnik house (2011) is to be built on the site of a former fishing camp in Saugerties, New York, on a promontory of land jutting into the Hudson River. Smith and Thompson based the layout and spirit of this vacation house on early "Carpenter Gothic" houses by Andrew Jackson Downing who placed windows and bracketed porches to frame views of picturesque rural scenes, just as the Hudson River School of artists had done in their paintings. The architects' plan calls for three separate living pavilions--a living/dining space, a master bedroom suite, and a children's pavilion--linked together by a central pathway and series of terraces, to be built with lightweight steel framing, timber ceiling joists, recycled decking material and sedum-planted roofs. (The airy and elongated plan of multiple parts is reminiscent of their proposal for the East Hampton Airport.) Each of the glass-sheathed pavilions will enjoy expansive and uninterrupted views up and down the river. All floors are made from stained and polished concrete with radiant heating. A pre-existing fishing cabin that sits on a bluff in front of the house is being restored for future use as a pool house.

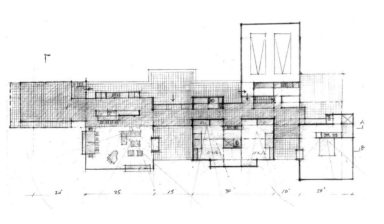

The program for the Gordon/De Vries house and studio (2006) presented an exercise in dualities, a chance to explore the ever-diminishing line between domestic frontiers and work routines, between "downtime" and "uptime," and what it means to escape the city while still being plugged in to a far-reaching digital network. These dualities were graphically expressed in the simple salt-and-pepper-shaker scheme, keeping new and old as distinct elements, the 18th-century farmhouse clad in white clapboard versus the modern section clad in rough-hewn, horizontal pine stained black.

An hour and a half northwest of New York City, the original house was a small, weekend getaway perched high on the side of a hill overlooking two converging streams. The owners--a writer and a designer (and authors of this book)--wanted to expand it into a year-round residence and workplace, big and flexible enough for themselves and their four children. They desired open, light-filled spaces but also wanted to retain the historic feeling of the original structure. The idea was quite simple: celebrate the best of both worlds, retain the cozy comfort of the timber-frame homestead and marry it to an urban, loft-like expansion.

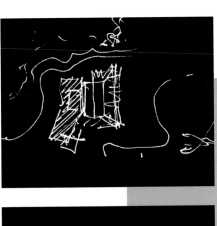

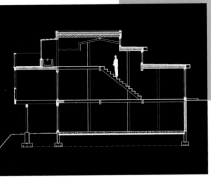

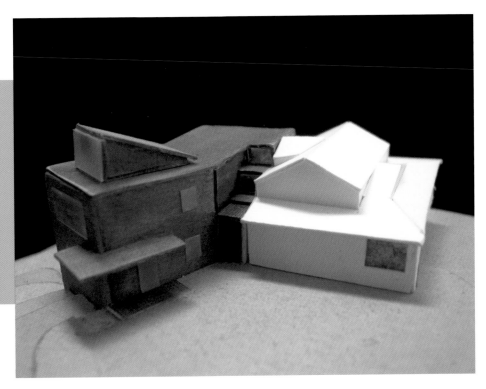

PAGE 174:
The new entrance

PAGE 175:
New addition behind the old house

LEFT:
New entrance hallway

OPPOSITE:
Open plan kitchen

An early 20th century dining room and kitchen were demolished and the house was stripped down to its 18th century bones with meticulously restored hand-hewn beams, rafters and a massive stone fireplace. A modern, three-story block was added with approximately 5,000 square feet of additional live/work space including studios and storage on the lowest level, a single large dining space living areas on the main floor with bedrooms and an office on the third level.

Going against the prevailing trend in off-site prefabrication, a concerted effort was made to use local materials, local labor and recycled elements whenever possible. New floorboards were milled from local pine by a nearby sawmill. Exterior ough pine cladding was also locally milled. Part of the floor in the living room was hand made by the owners using disks of white oak cut from a dying tree on the property and set into concrete like cobblestones. (The idea came from a floor in Robert Motherwell's Chareau-designed Quonset house in East Hampton, N.Y.) Local Pennsylvania blue stone was used for terraces and entryways. Many elements from a previously owned property in New Jersey were recycled. A floating staircase made from aluminum I-beams and ash steps was unbolted and trucked to the site in Pennsylvania, as were translucent Lexan panels, steel shelving, a 19th century laundry sink and movable walls on an industrial tracking system.

OPPOSITE:
Porch overlooking stream

ABOVE:
Addition seen from stream

RIGHT:
Sketch of addition

PAGES 180-181:
View from the old house into the addition, plan of first floor and 200 year old fireplace

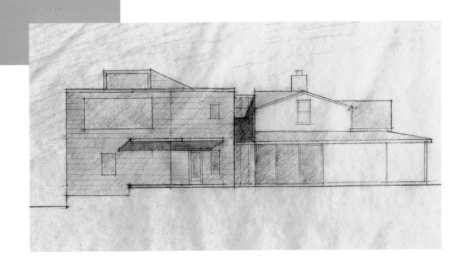

A cube-shaped addition created a new entry sequence and was angled by the architects to follow the contours of the land and negotiate a steep drop towards the streambed below. A sloping, light monitor rises from the flat roof of this section and echoes the sloping roof of the old house. Structural members were prefabricated beams laminated with steel plates left raw and exposed, in a sense matching the exposed woodwork of the original house but acknowledging new methodologies. Large areas of glass were used on the north side of the house for optimal views and to provide generous light for the owners' two studios. A wide, screened-in living porch reaches out over the stream and opens up the interiors to the encroaching forest.

PAGE 182:
View from addition into old
dining room

PAGE 183:
Handmade wood inlay floor

LEFT:
The addition at dusk

186

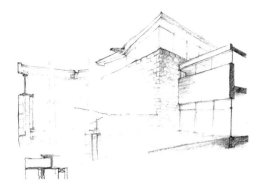

In 2008, Smith and Thompson began designing an encampment for the Krauss family to be built on a five-acre, rocky site at the end of a long rustic lane, overlooking South Spectacle Lake in Kent, Connecticut. The project is to be fairly grand in scope, comprising a total of 12,500 square feet of space including four separate housing structures for the extended Krauss family that would be linked by three circulation towers and glass-enclosed galleries. The master plan included a four-car garage, a caretaker's cottage, a gym and swimming pool. The main structure will be set on a high point of land and nestled into the rocky hillside. All rooms are given special views of the lake, recalling the site planning effects of the Jacques Marchais Museum with minimal elevation exposure to the arrival side and high glazed elevations facing south and views of the lake. (Local covenants required a 300-foot scenic setback from the lake as well as the preservation of all trees over a certain caliper.) Stone from the excavation process will be used to create the outer veneer of the house and recall the traditional fieldstone walls of Connecticut. Stucco and mahogany will be used for trim and detailing.

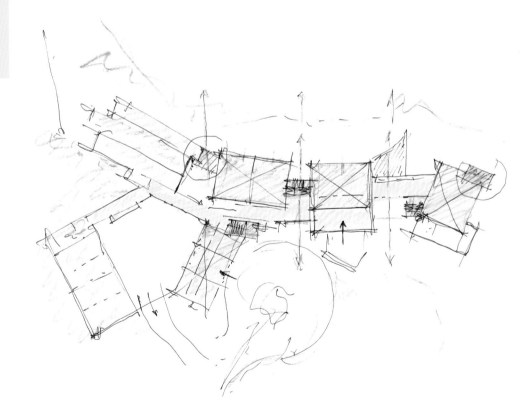

OPPOSITE, ABOVE:
Rendering,
Krauss Residence,
South Spectacle Lake,
Kent, Connecticut, 2010

BOTH PAGES:
Elevation, detail and
plan sketches of Krauss
Residence

PAGES 188-189:
Smith and Thompson
Residence, East Hampton,
New York, 2010

ABOVE:
Original structure, 1987

BELOW:
Thompson (left) and Smith at
site, 1989

OPPOSITE, LEFT:
Stages of evolution

OPPOSITE, RIGHT:
Model of architect's
residence

For several years Smith and Thompson were looking for a site to build a modern house in East Hampton, N.Y., when they came across a property on Spring Close Highway near the LIRR railway. They saw possibilities in working with the existing buildings: a 1920s tractor barn with a smaller potato barn attached that had already been converted to a residence by the previous owner. They bought the property in 1987 and began a gradual process of reclamation and expansion that would stretch over twenty-three years. Indeed, the property would become something like a laboratory workshop in slow design, a place where the architects could try out new ideas, change directions and practice living with the results.

In the first phase of remodeling, Smith and Thompson opened up the south facing gable of the old potato barn and replaced it with sheer glass. They created a simple living area and kitchen and made a narrow, ladder-like staircase that lead to a sleeping loft. They moved in and allowed the rest of the building to evolve organically over the next twenty years. The smaller barn was internally connected to the larger barn with its gabled roof running lengthwise. White walls and window trim of the old barns would tie in with the new additions that are all white with large glazed openings. The house becomes more fractured and abstracted as the composition pulls eastwards, like a slow train, toward the main entry.

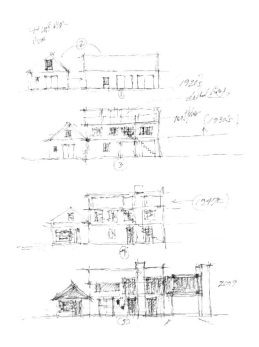

By breaking up forms into discreet cubic entities, the architects mediated the scale and mood of the rustic barns with the bolder additions and incorporated them as integral parts of the composition. The overall effect is pastoral and inviting while suggesting a certain degree of secrecy and restraint. New additions are flat roofed, open and transparent, contrasting with the older sections which are gabled and more opaque with shingle siding. The pitched roofs and shingled walls of the old barns become abstract elements in the overall composition--one thinks of Charles Sheeler's Precisionist paintings of barns in Bucks County--with subtle gradations, planes intersecting other planes, overlapping shadows, muted colors, small dark windows surrounded by clapboard, rustic doors rolling back on overhead tracks, deep eaves, bright patches of sunlight, all of it together, telling a story without words.

A long bay window in the living room cantilevers out on either side of the main chimney and is broken up with vertical mullions, recalling José Luis Sert's renovated carriage house (1949) on Long Island. The dining-and-kitchen pavilion floats as a bridge between the old and new sections of the house and is articulated by yet another bay with a narrow deck that hangs above the entry courtyard. A light tower rises high above the kitchen and draws natural light from every direction. Moving further eastwards, a glassed-in stairwell rises twenty-four feet as a final exclamation point. (This was the maximum height allowed by local zoning regulations for a flat-roofed structure.) The transparent tower structure gives access to the second floor and continues up to a roof deck outside the third floor.

RIGHT:
Original entrance and new bay window

PAGE 194:
Cantilevered east facade

PAGE 195:
Entrance and dining pavilion

OPPOSITE:
View of stair tower
from dining space

RIGHT:
Exterior of stair tower

PAGE 198, LEFT:
First floor studio window

PAGE 198-199:
West façade with flying
bridge

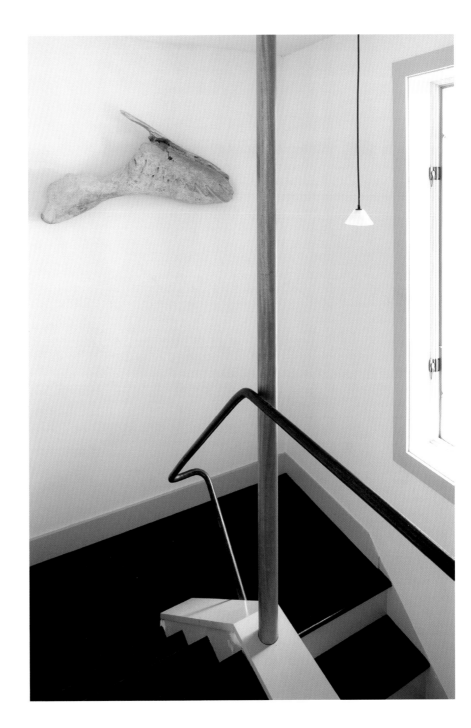

While expanding the main residence, Smith and Thompson also designed and built a small pool house, something like a garden folly and Japanese teahouse combined. This structure was originally designed in 1989 and the footings, concrete walls and steel arbor were built over the next three years. It was not until 2007 that the architects resumed work on the project, and after reconsidering the original design, felt it was still the strongest solution.

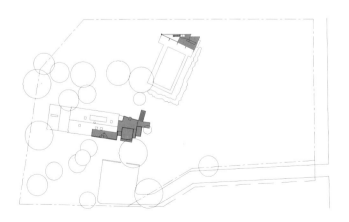

Working with office staff, they framed out the structure themselves under the direction of Abe Argibay, a long-term architectural assistant and master carpenter. The second level was finished with a shutter system fabricated in the Yucatan Peninsula of Mexico.

The pool house, in a sense, completed the property and provided a meditative retreat, changing spaces, an inside/outside fireplace and a bathroom. "We wanted a dialogue between the two buildings," said Smith, who explained how the structure was designed in accordance with three basic conditions: the setback from the northern property line, the alignment of the pre-existing swimming pool and a local pyramid zoning law that determined the shape of the sod roof.

"The south-facing pavilion was raised so that its bulk would float above the existing hedges and provide a shaded poolside area," he said.

The upper level of the pool house rests on narrow steel pilotis and hangs out over the terrace and pool. A steel and mahogany ladder leads up beside a concrete wall and into a small meditation room with a sculptural fireplace, an experience that recalls the kampong houses of Malaysia. Because of such a steep slope, the sod roof posed something of a challenge. The weight of the roof created a substantial horizontal force resolved by the steel arbor that acts something like the buttresses of a Gothic cathedral. The architects also needed a way to restrain the sod so that it wouldn't slip down the steep pitch of the roof. In Scandinavia, the roofs would traditionally be restrained by securing horizontal battens at regular intervals. Smith and Thompson developed a similar approach and secured three-inch aluminum angles at twenty-four-inch intervals that also served as the scaffolding for the installation process. Holes were drilled through the aluminum to allow the passage of rainwater. Then they cut pieces of sod that were four inches deep and one foot square in their orchard and carried them on plywood trays up to the roof. It took a day and a half to complete the installation. The natural enclosure of the hedge running along the back of the property was effectively extended by the architectural forms of the building. The sod roof and vine-covered trellis further engaged the natural setting. "Certain geometric aspects of the building, such as the chimney/skylight, were juxtaposed against natural forms and reminded us of the eternal debate between the Romantic and the Classical," said Smith. A one-hundred-foot-long Corten steel garden wall completes the northern boundary of the property.

PAGES 204-205:
Pool House with sod roof

OPPOSITE:
Stair and railing detail and
entry door porthole

ABOVE:
Cedar shutters made in the
Yucatan

RIGHT:
Concrete table and fireplace

LEFT:
Interior of Pool House

PAGES 210-211:
House at dusk

OPPOSITE:

Family Retreat, Eleuthera, the
Bahamas, 2012
A sequence of camp-like
pavilions descends from the
brow of a hill towards the
Atlantic Ocean, hovering in
the cradle of the lush semi-
tropical landscape. Water
collection cisterns, solar
electric generators as well
as wind turbines make the
compound self-sufficient

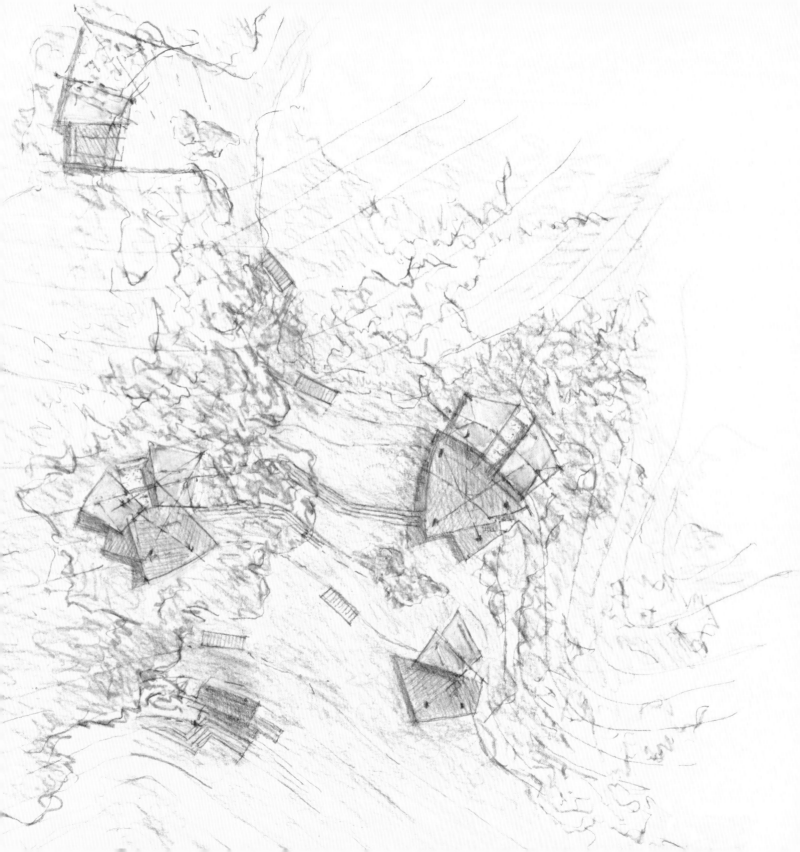

Acknowledgements

Collaboration has been our studio's modus operandi and we wish to thank all of our clients and associates who have shared the value of this approach: William and Lucy Friedman (on five different projects), Barbara Lipton (former Director of the Tibetan Museum), Bob Moribe, Nancy Okada, Toyo Kukuchi, Cherryl Ikema (New York Buddhist Church), Paul Robinson, Robert and Janie Fisher, Elizabeth and Bruce Resnik, Rick and Natasha Stowe, Robert Kleeb, Franca and Fiona Lally, Pat Rudick and her son Daniel, Janos, Helen and Christopher Scholz, Peter G. Davis, Lida Orzeck and Susan Miller, Jeffrey Krauss and Debby Vilas, Gerard Debenedetto and Fangya Jiang, Alastair Gordon and Barbara de Vries, Richard Schoenfeldt and Karen Young, Steve and Lillian Brash, Jock Pottle and Paula Balboni, Steve and Sue Simring, as well as many others.

We would also like to acknowledge the craftspeople, builders and consultants who have been an integral part of the Smith and Thompson team: contractors Kevin Sullivan and Tyreik Jackson, Arlen Haruthunian, Bruce Sherman, Mark Jones, Anthony Cantanzaro, John Radigan, cabinetmakers David Smolen and George Berdeja, mastercraftsman Abe Argibay, metalworker David Johnson, Joe and Jerry at E & J Ironworks, Jim Svendsen Steel Works, Metalworks Inc., Milgo/Bufkin, Frank Scafuri at Barrasso and Sons, pre-cast concrete, Hisao and Zui Hanafusa at Mija Shoji, Leon Breuer of Langsam and Breuer, Robin Key, Margarate Rudick and Judith Heinzt, Landscape Architects, Conor Sampson, lighting designer, David Harvey, acoustical and Paul Gossen, Lin Levine, Linden Schulz, Steve Maresca, John Fuller, Robert Silman and Joe Sage, engineers.

We value our assistants and interns and have had continuing relationships with many over the years. During the past decade we have sponsored a unique internship program with foreign exchange students from Eindhoven University of Technology in the Netherlands and the Bauhaus University in Weimar, Germany. We wish to thank: Abelardo Argibay, Robin Auchincloss, Erica Avrami, Adam Baz, Brian Berson, Daniel Bittiker, Olle Blomquist, Till Boettger, Jolien Bruin, Kevin Byrne, Schuyler Cadwalder, Sarah Calkins, Souhaib Chaabane, Tom Cordell, Javier de la Grazia, Sandro De Roma, Debbie Epstein, Gil Evan-Tsur, Mengyi Fan, Simon Fellmeth, Mary Fernando, Maaike Goedkoop, Arwin Goharani, Lars Goossens, Martin Grunewald, Yves Habegger, Ole Hallier, David Hong, Douglas Jones, Krzysztop Kaszuboxski, James Ke,

Michael Kearney, Katia Kevork, Oliver Kienzie, Eli King, Caroline Koot, Richard Kreshtool, Jun Kumazawa, Kevin Kunkle, Elizabeth Leber, Joris Lipsch, Bryan McNally, Pierre Milanini, Jochen Motruk, Dirk Osinga, Paul Paloglou, Ivo Piazza, Robert Pierpont, Michael Randazzo, Eric Robinson, Wouter Roemaat, Damijan Saccio, Evan Sagerman, Christopher Scholz, Simone Sexauer, Marshall Shuster, Tim Stenson, Gerjan Streng, Kevin Sweet, Julia Taylor, Olafur Thordarson, Peter Tow, Terry Van Dyne, Barry Van Emple, Christoph Wand, Susan Wedgel, Ulrick Wienert, Tal Yaar, Yvonne Yao, Caroline Zimmerle and Bradley Zizmore.

Over the years we have had the good fortune to work with exceptional photographers like Paul Warchol, Douglas Baz, Norman McGrath, Jock Pottle, Eric Freeland and Michael Moran and we wish to thank them for allowing us to use their beautiful work in this book.

A very special thanks goes to Gordon de Vries Studio. Working with Alastair Gordon and Barbara de Vries has been a source of enlightened discourse. We appreciate Alastair's insights into our architecture and his ability to make connections that even we weren't aware of, not to mention his lyrical prose. It has been equally illuminating to work with Barbara whose creative direction helped to pull forty years of work into a powerful visual narrative. Several assistants also helped with the design process and particular thanks go to Jolien Bruin, Maaike Goedkoop and Dirk Osinga.

Phillip Smith and Douglas Thompson

ABOVE:
Sketch of cliff and beach,
Eleuthera

List of Projects

Shunney Studio, Nantucket, MA, 1975

Booth Residence, Nantucket, MA, 1975

Howard Street Residence and Guest House, Nantucket, MA, 1975

Norman Residence, Nantucket, MA, 1975

Richmond Barn Renovation, Nantucket, MA, 1975

Webster Residence, Nantucket, MA, 1975

Nantucket Gallery, Nantucket, MA, 1975

Roosevelt Island Competition, Roosevelt Island, NYC, 1975

Phillipines Competition, Manilla, Phillipines, 1975

Thompson Apartment, East 91st Street, NYC, 1975

Cooperstown Hotel Renovation, Cooperstown, NY, 1976

Emmons Residence, Nantucket, MA, 1976

Pahlavi Library Competition, Teheran, Iran, 1977

Residential Tower, Cathedral Parkway, NYC, 1977

Smith Family Retreat, Blackwater Falls, WV, 1977

Gus's Restaurant, Broadway, NYC, 1977

Scholz Penthouse, Park Avenue, NYC, 1977

Shephard/Finch Townhouse, W. 94th Street, NYC, 1979

Payson Residence, Saratoga Springs, NY, 1979

West Residence, Pittsburg, PA, 1980

Banks Hunting Lodge, East Branch, NY, 1980

Carson Residence, Georgetown, SC, 1980

Carol Ross Loft, Chelsea, NYC, 1981

Colgazier Building, 7th Avenue South, NYC, 1981

Peter G. Davis Rooftop Addition, NYC, 1982

Rifkin Apartment, Greenwich Village, NYC, 1982

Orzeck/Alers Loft, Chelsea, NYC, 1982

Pierrepont Street Apartment House, Brooklyn Heights, NYC, 1982

Vershbow Townhouse, West 22nd Street, NYC, 1983

Greenberg/Zimmerman Townhouse, West 87th Street, NYC, 1983

Southmark Offices, Rockefeller Center, NYC, 1983

Weinstein Barn, Remsenburg, Long Island, NY, 1983

Woolams Townhouse, West 81st Street, NYC, 1984

Friedman Apartment, CPW, NY, 1984

Rudick Apartment, East 86th Street, NYC, 1984

Kennelly Loft, SoHo, NYC, 1984

Sullivan Townhouse, Brooklyn, NYC, 1984

Devi/Moschera Residence, Hasting, NY, 1984

Edwards Apartment, West 79th Street, NYC, 1984

Horan Townhouse, West 81st Street, NYC, 1985

Sherrin Loft, Tribeca, NYC, 1985

Commercial/Residential Building, East 59th Street, NYC, 1985

Dance Technology Disco, San Jose, CA, 1985

Norman Apartment, CPW, NY, 1985

Kleeb Apartment, Chelsea, NYC, 1985

Twin Loft/Penthouse Project, West 23rd Street, NYC, 1986

Ornstein, East 69th Street, NYC, 1986

Sherrin Office, Long Island City, NYC, 1986

Price Gallery, East 57th Street, NYC, 1986

Fendelman Loft, East 13th Street, NYC, 1986

Norman Apartment, CPW, NYC, 1986

Washington Square Apartments, NYC, 1987

Schaff Townhouse One, West 11th Street, NYC, 1987

Infill Housing, First phase, Cathedral Parkway, NYC, 1987

Kleeb Residence, East Hampton, NY, 1987

McVicker Apartment, Brooklyn, NYC, 1988

Johnson Apartment, West 81st Street, NYC, 1988

Schaff Townhouse Two, Barrow Street, NYC, 1988

D. Smith Penthouse Renovation, WEA, NYC, 1988

Friedman Residence, Seaview, Fire Island, NY, 1988

Townhouse, 13th Street, NYC, 1989

East Hampton Airport Competition, East Hampton, NY, 1989

SmithThompson Poolhouse, East Hampton, NY, 1989-2011

National Realty Offices, Madison Ave, NYC, 1990

C. E. Smith Residence, Mobile, AL, 1990

New York Buddhist Church, Riverside Drive, NYC, 1990

Pottle Rooftop Addition, West 81st Street, NYC, 1990

Mobile Government Center Competition, Mobile, AL, 1990

Yamaha Factory Master Plan, Nagoya, Japan, 1990

Newman Residence Addition, Bedford, NY, 1990

Graubard Residence, Larchmont, NY, 1991

Kleeb Residence, Santa Fe, NM, 1991

Brash Apartment, East 84th Street, NYC, 1991

Du Puis Apartment, East 96th Street, NYC, 1991

New York Buddhist Church, Phase I, Riverside Drive, NYC, 1992

Infill Housing Second Phase, 542 Cathedral Parkway, NYC, 1992

Sibley Loft, Irving Place, NYC, 1992

Spring Close Cottage, East Hampton, NY, 1992

Rudick Residence, Quogue, Long Island, NY, 1993

Gordon/DeVries Loft, Princeton, NJ, 1993

Lobby Renovation, East 84th Street, NYC, 1993

Siegel Residence, Red Hook, NY, 1994

Schaff Residence, Red Hook, NY, 1994

Tibetan Museum, Staten Island, NY, 1994

Montauk Day Care Center, Montauk, NY, 1994

Mc Namie Residence, Quogue, NY, 1994

Newborne Loft, West 17th Street, NYC, 1994

Orzeck/Miller Apartment, CPW, NYC, 1995

National Realty Offices, Park Avenue, NYC, 1995

Brash Residence, Quogue, NY, 1995

Yahr Apartment, WEA, NYC, 1995

Yahr Residence, Hastings, NY, 1995

ARF Doghouse, East Hampton, NY, 1996

Gallery Building, West 23rd Street, NYC, 1996

Warren Square Townhouses, Savannah, GA, 1996

Sorrentino Apartments, Milford, NY, 1996

Ughi/Frankel Penthouse, East 73rd Street, NYC, 1997

Lally Loft, West 55th Street, NYC, 1997

Spencer/Booker Loft, NoHo, NYC, 1997

Sunset Motel Addition, Key West, FL, 1997

Young Schoenfelt Townhouse, West 95th Street, NYC, 1997

Rudick Residence Two, Quogue, NY, 1998

Clark Stephan Loft, West 55th Street, NYC, 1998

Alshooler Townhouse, East 38th Street, NYC, 1998

Sackler/Pugh Penthouse Addition, Chelsea, NYC, 1998

Clark/Stephan Loft, West 55th Street, NYC, 1998

Denton Loft, Brooklyn, NYC, 1998

Pottle Residence, West 89th Street, NYC, 1999

Fisher Residence, Westhampton Beach, Long Island, NY, 1999

Benfield Loft, West 55th Street, NYC, 1999

Pearl Loft, 4th Avenue, NYC, 1999

Resnik Loft, 4th Avenue, NYC 2000

Casa Serrano, Highline, West 23rd Street, NYC 2000

Caravan Italian Language Institute, Master Plan, NYC, 2000

Caravan Italian Language Institute, Phase I, NYC, 2000

Youthstream Offices, Chrysler Centre, NYC, 2000

Tarragon Realty Offices, West 57th Street, NYC, 2000

Krauss Residence, East 88th Street, NYC, 2000

Ursus Art Books, West 21st Street, NYC, 2000

Caravan Italian Language Institute, Phase II, NYC, 2001

Pottle Residence, Phase Two, West 89th Street, NYC, 2001

Gordon/DeVries Residence, Amagansett, NY, 2001

Rudick Residence, Tower Restoration, Westhampton, NY, 2001

Ma Residence, 101st Street, NYC, 2001

Fisher Building, Façade and Lobby, East 46th Street, NYC, 2001

DeBenedetto/Jiang Loft, Charlton Street, NYC, 2001

Jessey Loft, West 23rd Street, NYC, 2002

Queens Museum of Art, Competition, Queens, NYC, 2002

Kempner Gallery, New Staircase, West 23rd Street, NYC, 2002

Gallery Building Addition, Chelsea, NYC, 2002

Rudick Residence, East 32nd Street, NYC, 2002

Gofran Building, Mixed Use Tower, Chittagong, BD, 2003-12

Resnik Residence, Jane Street, NYC, 2003

Lobby Renovation, West 55th Street, NYC, 2003

Zimmerman Residence, West 87th Street, NYC, 2003

Daniel Rudick Residence, Renovation, Westhampton, NY, 2003

Harper/Terruso Residence, Kent, CT, 2003

Highline Park Competition, NYC, 2003

Tarragon Realty Offices, West 54th Street, NYC, 2005

Fisher Residence, Easthampton, NY, 2005

Church of the Epiphany, Space Planning, York Ave, NYC, 2005

Gordon/DeVries Residence, Milford, PA, 2006

Church of the Epiphany, Competition, York Ave, NYC, 2006

Stowe Residence, Fifth Avenue, NYC, 2006

New York Buddhist Church, Sanctuary, Riverside Dr., NYC, 2008

Fendelman Loft Redeux, East 13th Street, NYC, 2009

Krauss Residence, Kent, CT, 2010

SmithThompson Residence, East Hampton, NY, 2010

Miami Seaplane Base, Competition, FL, 2010

Brash Residence, Quogue, NY, 2011

Resnik Residence, Saugerties, NY, 2011

Sagaponac House, Sagaponack, NY, 2011

Church of the Epiphany, Facility Study, York Ave, NYC, 2012

Simring Residence, Tenafly, NJ, 2012

New York Buddhist Church, Addition, Riverside Dr., NYC, 2012

Marfa House and Gallery, Marfa, TX, 2012

Family Compound, Eleuthera, The Bahamas, 2012

Residential Tower Project, West 23rd Street, NYC, 2012

Smith and Thompson Architects 2011
Left to right: Phillip Smith, Jolien Bruin, Marshall Shuster,
Douglas Thompson, Julia Taylor, Maaike Goedkoop and
Abelardo Argibay

Photos and illustrations

End Notes

1.   Luis Barragan, Laureate Acceptance Speech, The Pritzker Architecture Prize, 1980.

2.   See: Sally Woodbridge, *Bernard Maybeck, Visionary Architect*. New York: Abbeville Press, 1992, 129.

3.   During the continuing recession of the late 1970s, Thompson worked with Mitchell Giurgola Architects while simultaneously collaborating with Smith.

4.   See: Alastair Gordon, *Weekend Utopia: Modern Living in the Hamptons*. New York: Princeton Architectural Press, 2000.

5.   Alastair Gordon, " The Terminal Without Politics," *East Hampton Star*, October 26, 1989.

6.   Suzanne Slesin, " The East Hampton Intercontinental Airport Contest," *New York Times*, June 29, 1989.

7.   De Benedetto/Jiang Loft, New York City, NY, 2001.

8.   Haus-Rucker-Co, *Rooftop Oasis Project: Tenant's Guide to Organizing Rooftop Projects*, Caroll Michels ed., New York, 1976, 3.

9.   "New York May Waive Zoning for New Apartments," *New York Times*, June 19, 1977.

10.   See: Robert A.M. Stern; David Fishman; Jacob Tilove. *New York 2000: Architecture and Urbanism from the Bicentennial to the Millenium*. New York: Monacelli Press, 2006, 45-46. "The Smith and Thompson team proposed a Modernist design which picked up on the ideas put forth by the 1985 Columbia study, providing workshop spaces at the rear of the site that would inject economic activity into the project. The Smith and Thompson proposal called for masonry bearing walls that were relatively inexpensive and could be built by semiskilled laborers."

11.   See: Alastair Gordon, " Making Manhattan an Island of Calm," *New York Times*, November 18, 1999.